BIBLE 101

SIX SESSIO[NS]

MW00364524

TIMES & PLACES

Picturing the events of the Bible

WILLOW CREEK RESOURCES

mIcHaeL ReDDINg

BILL DONAHUE. SERIES EDITOR

IVP

InterVarsity Press
Downers Grove, Illinois
Leicester, England

InterVarsity Press
P.O. Box 1400, Downers Grove, IL 60515
World Wide Web: www.ivpress.com
E-mail: mail@ivpress.com

Inter-Varsity Press, England
38 De Montfort Street, Leicester LE1 7GP, England

InterVarsity Press® is the book-publishing division of InterVarsity Christian Fellowship/USA®, a student movement active on campus at hundreds of universities, colleges and schools of nursing in the United States of America, and a member movement of the International Fellowship of Evangelical Students. For information about local and regional activities, write Public Relations Dept., InterVarsity Christian Fellowship/USA, 6400 Schroeder Rd., P.O. Box 7895, Madison, WI 53707-7895.

Inter-Varsity Press, England, is the book-publishing division of the Universities and Colleges Christian Fellowship (formerly the Inter-Varsity Fellowship), a student movement linking Christian Unions in universities and colleges throughout the United Kingdom and the Republic of Ireland, and a member movement of the International Fellowship of Evangelical Students. For information about local and national activities write to UCCF, 38 De Montfort Street, Leicester LE1 7GP.

Cover design: Grey Matter Group

Photo image: Photodisc

Chapter icons: Roberta Polfus

USA ISBN 0-8308-2062-0

UK ISBN 0-85111-533-0

Printed in the United States of America ∞

16	15	14	13	12	11	10	9	8	7	6	5	4	3	2	1
12	11	10	09	08	07	06	05	04	03	02	01	00			

Contents

Introduction

Some time ago, Russ Robinson (director of small group ministries at Willow Creek Community Church and concept editor on these guides) and I were talking about how to help groups get a firm grip on the Word of God. Both of us had studied and taught courses on the Bible, but what about small groups? What if we could put something together that could be studied as a group and yet have much of the information people would normally find in a class or course? Well, hats off to Russ, who came up with the idea for Bible 101 and cast the vision for what it could look like. Soon we were outlining the books, and the result is what you have before you. So welcome to the Bible 101 adventure, a place where truth meets life!

Traditionally the subject matter in this series has been reserved for classroom teaching or personal study. Both are places where this curriculum could be used. But this work is primarily targeted at small groups, places where men and women, old and young, rich and poor gather together in community to engage fully with the truth of God's Word. These little communities can be transforming in ways that classrooms and personal study cannot.

Few things in life are more fulfilling than drawing out the deep truths of Scripture and then seeing them at work to change a life into the image of Christ. Getting a firm grip on the Bible and its teachings is paramount to a mature and intelligent walk with God. We are to worship him with all our heart, soul, mind and strength. And the Word of God is central to accomplishing God's desire that we be fully devoted to him.

The team from Willow Creek—staff and volunteers alike—has labored diligently to provide you with a group-friendly process for understanding the Bible. Kathy Dice, Gerry Mathisen, Judson Poling, Michael Redding and I have worked to provide something that merges content and process, learning and application. Now it is up to you to work together to discover the riches that lie ahead for those willing to do some work and take a few risks. But we know you are more than ready for that challenge!

To make these studies more productive, here are a few suggestions and guidelines to help you along the way. Read carefully so that you get the most out of this series.

Purpose

This series is designed to ground a Christ-follower in the study and understanding of Scripture. It is not designed for someone who became a Christian last week, though sections of it would certainly be good. And it is not as rigorous as a Bible college class or seminary course might be. Bible 101 means *foundational,* but not easy or light. So be prepared for some challenge and some stretching. This may be the first time you are exposed to certain theological concepts or terms, or to some more in-depth methods of Bible study. Celebrate the challenge and strive to do your best. Peter tells us to "make every effort" to add knowledge to our faith. It will take some effort, but I can guarantee it will be well worth it!

Prayer

When approaching the Word of God you will need to keep a submissive and teachable attitude. The Holy Spirit is eager to teach you, but you must be willing to receive knowledge, encouragement, correction and challenge. One educator has taught that all learning is the result of failed expectations. We hope that in some ways you are ambushed by the truth and stumble upon new and unfamiliar territory that startles you into new ways of thinking about God and relating to him through Christ.

Practice

Each session has the same format, except (in some cases) the last session. For five meetings you will learn skills, discuss material and readings, work together as a team, and discover God's truths in fresh and meaningful ways. The sixth session will be an opportunity to put all you have learned into practice. Studies are designed as follows.

 Establishing Base Camp (5-10 minutes). A question or icebreaker to focus the meeting.

 Mapping the Trail (5-10 minutes). An overview of where we are headed.

 Beginning the Ascent (30 minutes). The main portion of the discussion time.

Gaining a Foothold (3 minutes). Information to read that identifies core issues and ideas to keep you on track with the journey.

 Trailmarkers (10 minutes). Important Scriptures for memorization or reflection.

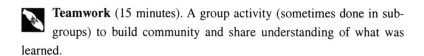 **Teamwork** (15 minutes). A group activity (sometimes done in subgroups) to build community and share understanding of what was learned.

 Reaching the Summit (5 minutes). A chance to summarize and look back at what has been learned or accomplished.

Close in Prayer (as long as you want!). An opportunity to pray for one another and ask God to deepen the truths of Scripture in you.

You can take some shortcuts or take longer as the group decides, but strive to stay on schedule for a 75- to 90-minute meeting, including prayer time. You will also want to save time to attend to personal needs. This will vary by group and can also be accomplished in personal relationships you develop between meetings.

Preparation

Preparation? There is none! Well, almost none. For some sessions reading ahead will be suggested to provide an overview. But the sessions are designed to be worked through together. We find this builds a sense of team and community, and is also more fun! And there is something about "discovery in the moment" rather than merely discussing what everyone has already discovered outside the meeting that provides a sense of adventure.

We wish you the best as you draw truth from the Word of God for personal transformation, group growth and kingdom impact!

Bill Donahue, Series Editor
Vice President, Small Group Ministries
Willow Creek Association

Session 1

Geography of the Bible

Discovering Middle Eastern culture.

Establishing Base Camp

My first memories of being able to recognize places came from a series of books lying on our coffee table at home. These colorful books depicted the American Civil War. Places I had visited as a child (though I barely remembered some of them) came alive when I saw them from a bird's-eye view, complete with drawings of soldiers on battlefields, roads, barns, rivers and houses. I learned much of what I know about our country from studying these maps and tracing the movement of the Union and Confederate troops.

Nearly two thousand years ago, a man named Ptolemy made a map of the world—as he understood it. He made some guesses and labeled the parts that had not been explored as *Terra Incognita,* "the Unknown Land." Using maps like this and thinking China and India to be much closer to Europe than they in fact were, a young explorer set out and sailed west to find the east. His name was Christopher Columbus, and the rest, as they say, "is geography" (as told by Kiernan O'Mahoney, *Geographical Literacy*).

Geography, it turns out, is a lot more than looking at a map! The events recorded in the Bible by and large took place in and around the Middle East, a small strip of land at the eastern end of the Mediterranean Sea (see map 1). Imagine for a few minutes that all the events in the history of the world had taken place in your own state or county. The very spot on which you are sitting would have been the site of thousands of events, each justifying its own historical marker. The terrain would have remained the same except for any urbanization and industrialization.

The Holy Land could easily fit into the state of Florida—several times over. The distance from Jerusalem to the Mediterranean Sea (roughly thirty-five miles) is slightly longer than the distance across major metropolitan centers such as New York City, Chicago or London. Today such a distance could be covered in less than an hour (apart from rush hour traffic).

The densely inhabited region of Egypt where the Nile River empties into the Mediterranean Sea would occupy an area the size of the states of Massachusetts and Connecticut. Paul traveled to lands that span from the northern side of the Mediterranean Sea to Italy and Greece, as well as some islands. And the Old Testament story begins not far from the Persian Gulf, near present day Kuwait, Iran and Iraq. Yet from the Persian Gulf to Italy (including North Africa, the Mediterranean Sea and southern Turkey) you have an area little more than two-thirds the size of the United States. Imagine thousands of years of biblical history all taking place in that area!

✓ Without using modern location and travel resources (that is, GPS, maps, mileage markers, major highways) and modern transportation methods (cars, trains, buses or airplanes) describe to others how would you undertake a journey from your church to the nearest large metropolitan area.

Mapping the Trail

Let's begin with getting a lay of the land in the Bible, particularly during the Old Testament era.

The Old Testament Period

The majority of Old Testament narratives occurred in three regions that are together called the ancient Near East or the Fertile Crescent. Notice if you follow the map from Canaan north to Haran, east to Assyria and south to Ur, it forms a crescent-moon shape. Review three major geographical areas as you look at map 1.

1. The Holy Land. This region, also called Israel or Palestine, is the land

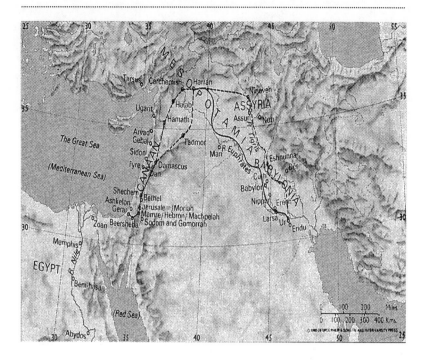

Map 1. Old Testament—the ancient Near East

between the eastern end of the Mediterranean Sea and the Jordan River. In the days of Abraham to Joshua it was called Canaan. Many people traveled through this area because it functioned as a land bridge that connected Europe, Africa and Asia.

2. Egypt. This long country follows the Nile from the shores of the Mediterranean southward to the mountains of Sudan.

3. Mesopotamia. This land, located in the heart of the Tigris and Euphrates River valley, is called the land of the Chaldees. Later it is known as Babylon, now modern-day Iraq.

✔ When you think of the Middle East, Babylon and Jerusalem, what images of the landscape come to mind?

✔ How have news events in the Middle East affected how you picture that area?

Beginning the Ascent

Read through "Basic Geographic Characteristics." Consult the maps listed as you read and answer the questions. Try to get a feel for the landscape and the environment.

Basic Geographic Characteristics

1. Natural features

A. *Coastal plains/fertile valleys (see map 1).* While the location of Eden is unknown, it may likely have been in Mesopotamia ("land between the rivers"). For this reason the valley of the Tigris and Euphrates Rivers is known as the "cradle of civilization." Except for the first chapters of Genesis, Mesopotamia does not figure significantly in the lives of major Old Testament characters, except as a point of departure for Abraham and as a place of captivity for those who were exiled from their land.

B. *(Once) forested hills and mountains (see map 2).* Great Britain, once heavily wooded, was severely deforested by Viking invaders more than one thousand years ago. Likewise much of Israel is today barren and rocky, but two thousand to three thousand years ago, large areas were forested.

C. *The Jordan Valley, where the Jordan River lies below sea level (map 2).* The Jordan River flows year round from north of the Sea of

> "But the land you are crossing the Jordan to take possession of is a land of mountains and valleys that drinks rain from heaven. It is a land the LORD your God cares for; the eyes of the LORD your God are continually on it from the beginning of the year to its end" (Deuteronomy 11:11-12).

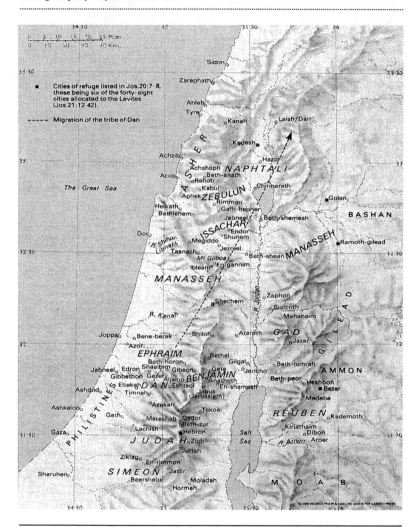

Map 2. The land of Canaan, divided among the twelve tribes

Galilee to the Dead Sea. Spring runoffs force the Jordan to flood stage, keeping the Jordan Valley a lush and green area. The surrounding area includes the regions to the southwest between Israel and Egypt (the Sinai Peninsula) and the regions east of the River Jordan (the kingdom of Jordan today).

D. Rocky, wilderness regions (see maps 1 and 2). Such regions are highly dependent on annual rainfall for vegetation. The repeated famines in Palestine were due to lack of rainfall, forcing Abraham and subsequent generations to seek food elsewhere. These wilderness regions were also places where Jesus met Satan (Matthew 4) or found solitude.

> Scriptures describing the biblical landscape include:
> • **fertile valleys with cultivated fields—Numbers 13:23-30**
> • **forested hills—Joshua 17:15, 18**
> • **rocky wilderness—Deuteronomy 1:19**
> • **village and cities—Genesis 11:27-31**

2. Humanly Created Features

A. Small towns, villages and rural communities. Abraham and his descendants lived a nomadic life. After the Israelites first took possession of the Promised Land (Joshua 3—12), the region was divided among the twelve tribal groups, based on existing towns and the adjacent fields (Joshua 13—21). They conquered the land gradually to prevent it from once again becoming a wilderness of uncultivated places (see Deuteronomy 7:22; 8:6-18). Their calendar of festivals followed the agricultural cycles.

B. Urban centers. Almost all the cities in the Old Testament were situated near mountaintops and high ridges with springs or wells nearby.

✔ Why would these features be important to the Old Testament characters?

While the ancient cities of the biblical world may not have reached the scale of our modern world-class cities—like Mexico City, London, New York—they furnished an important backdrop for the events that occurred in them. Urban centers would be the seat of the local and national governments as well as the centers of industry, learning and culture.

Old Testament Places to Know

Shechem	Sodom and Gomorrah
Ur	Jerusalem
Babylon	Haran
Canaan	Egypt
Assyria	Nineveh
Mediterranean Sea	Jordan River
Dead Sea (Salt Sea)	Persian Gulf (southeast of Ur)
Red Sea	Tigris River
Euphrates River	

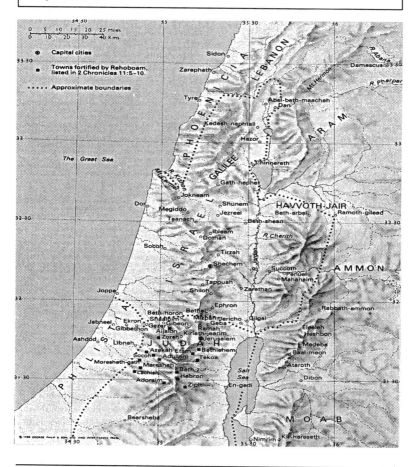

Map 3. Kingdoms of Israel and Judah

Let's look at maps 1, 2 and 3 to get familiar with the Old Testament landscape.

On maps 1 and 2 locate the places and bodies of water listed on page 15. You will better understand the Old Testament narratives and journeys if you get a handle on these important locations.

On map 2 notice the territories claimed by the twelve tribes after the conquest of Canaan by Joshua.

On map 3 notice how God's people once united under David became divided after Solomon's death (1 Kings 12). Israel became the people of the north and Judah controlled the south. Trace the boundaries of these kingdoms.

Note: Later, Jerusalem would be destroyed and God's people would be taken into exile (605 B.C., see Jeremiah 25:8-11). It would be seventy years later (about 535 B.C.) that they would be free to return again. It was not until the time of Ezra and Nehemiah (458 B.C.), however, that they finally arrive in Jerusalem and rebuild the temple. The Old Testament story ends about four hundred years before Christ is born, with God's people living all over the Middle East, some fully returning to Palestine, others scattered about the region. As we enter the New Testament period, the Romans, having taken control from the Greeks after Alexander the Great, are in control.

New Testament Period

The condition of the land remained fairly constant through the time of Christ. Some cities were destroyed or changed names over the years, partly as a result of the many battles with invaders from the north and east (Assyrians, Babylonians, Persians and Greeks). As we look at the New Testament geography, we move from the Promised Land to the west as Christianity spreads throughout the Roman Empire.

The New Testament events occurred during a period of approximately one hundred years, compared to the two thousand-plus years of the Old Testament story from Abraham to Jesus. The Old Testament's drama occupied three primary locations—Babylon, Canaan and Egypt. The New Testament focuses on Jesus' ministry in Israel and then flings the doors wide open to a large number of Mediterranean locations. We will focus on two regions for our maps—Jesus' life and ministry, and the ministry of Paul as the church spread north and west.

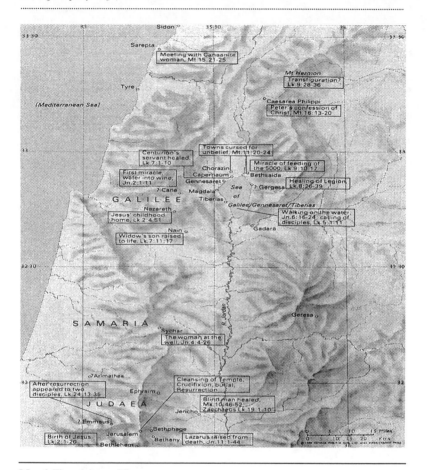

Map 4. The ministry of Jesus

New Testament Places to Know

These are some of the key places in New Testament history. By the time we are done, you should be able to locate them on maps 4 and 5.

Bethlehem	Nazareth
Samaria	Judea
Jerusalem	Asia, Macedonia and Achaia
Rome	Antioch (in Syria)
Sea of Galilee	Jordan River
Mediterranean Sea	Aegean Sea (west of Asia)

Look at map 4. Jesus' public ministry centered in two places, Galilee (the northern rural district), and Judea (mainly Jerusalem, the national capital). His trips to Jerusalem were infrequent in the beginning and coincided with national festivals. Later, his trips were more frequent and culminated with his arrest, crucifixion and resurrection.

Jesus' followers spread the good news about him in ever widening circles. Jesus made a statement about their activity, recorded in Acts 1:8. Though they did not immediately spread the message, persecution sent Jesus' followers throughout the land (Acts 8:1-4).

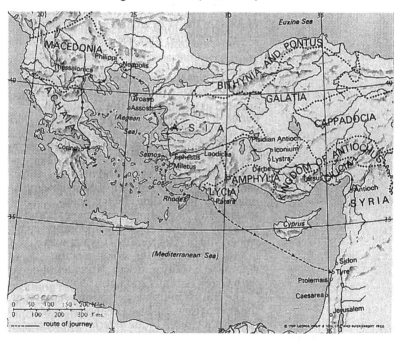

Map 5. Paul's Aegean ministry

Paul, after being converted on the Damascus Road (Acts 9), carries the gospel to the far reaches of the world (Acts 13—28). Map 5 outlines one of his missionary journeys. If you have a study Bible or Bible atlas (such as the *New Bible Atlas*) you can review additional, detailed maps showing Paul's journeys.

Trailmarkers

Read Genesis 12:1-3 and 17:8, noticing that the land given to Abram (Abraham) was one of God's promises of his covenant relationship with his people. You should be able to identify this land and see it's strategic importance to God's plan for the world.

Read Exodus 3:7-8 and note the description of the land. This land signifies three things: prosperity, blessing and freedom. Throughout the Old Testament, "Egypt" becomes a metaphor for slavery and idolatry (Isaiah 30:1-3), while God's Promised Land, specifically Jerusalem, is a place of redemption, hope and blessing (Psalm 122).

Read Acts 1:8 and identify the regions listed on maps 4 and 5. This passage is a great one to memorize. You could begin now, or commit it to memory as part of your own devotion and growth.

Teamwork

Turn to Acts 7. Stephen, before being stoned to death because of his faith in Christ, defends himself against his accusers. Break into two groups and identify a reader for each group. Read this aloud to your group and together identify places that are mentioned on the maps we studied (maps 1-3). Not all are listed on the maps, but many are. Notice how geography and chronology are used in Stephen's defense.

✓ Why does he spend so much time giving this history of Israel?

Reaching the Summit

You have covered a lot of territory in this session (literally!) and should feel a sense of accomplishment. You have not simply looked at maps; you have been tracing the work of God in the life of his people. And you have become more familiar with the world of the Bible. Take a moment to share any new insights you have discovered as a result of this session.

Next Session

In one or two minutes, how would you summarize your life over the last ten years?

Close in Prayer

Keep in mind the places we studied were home to people whose lives and deeds were recorded for our benefit. Challenges they faced in their culture impacted who they became. Ask God's help with the challenges that you face in this day and time.

Session 2

Creation to Law

Identifying and understanding the significance of key events in the lives of God's people, from creation to the giving of the Ten Commandments.

 ### Establishing Base Camp

Some years ago my wife was given a family tree showing all the characters of the Bible, a veritable genealogy of Adam and Eve. Even though my own name does not appear, I'm sure there is a connection somewhere. Actually my family's history is relatively obscure, but my mother has assured me many times that she is descended from the Winslows of the Mayflower colony. The discussion usually includes appropriate regret that our family no longer owns Martha's Vineyard!

Human history is in reality a compilation of life stories. It is said that the past is prologue, that decisions and activities of our ancestors form the backdrop of our lives. Though we may not know what they have said or done, we reflect the consequences of their choices and actions.

✓ How far back can you trace your family's history? Can you identify great events or great individuals?

✓ How did these events shape your family's history and your life? Which events do you think will have the greatest impact on your descendants?

Mapping the Trail

Each person's history is a mere dot on the drama of human history. Despite our seeming insignificance, it is clear that one decision, one action or one life can change the course of human history.

✓ In your opinion, what event in the early history of the Bible has had the most impact? Consider the period between creation and the Ten Commandments. Don't look at the Bible.

Beginning the Ascent

Let's walk through some of the key events in the early history of the Bible. As you move through these events together, try to keep the chronological flow of these in mind.

1. Creation of the world (Genesis 1—2). Read the creation story in Genesis 1:1—2:3 (especially 1:3, 6, 9, 14, 20, 27 and 2:2) and note God's activity on each day.

Day 1	Day 2	Day 3	Day 4	Day 5	Day 6	Day 7

2. The human race falls into sin (Genesis 3—6). When the man and woman rebelled against God, the results were devastating. In pairs, read Genesis 3:14-24 and list at least three consequences of their sin.

1. _____

2. _____

3. _____

✓ How do you see these consequences affecting us today?

3. The flood and Noah (Genesis 6—9). Sin continued to spread and devastate the earth. God, in his holiness, was forced to judge the Earth, but he spared Noah and his family because they had sought to live a godly life (7:1).

> **We too have been "uprooted" and "reestablished" in a new "place" because of what Christ has done on our behalf. "For he has rescued us from the dominion of darkness and brought us into the kingdom of the Son he loves, in whom we have redemption, the forgiveness of sins." (Colossians 1:13-14)**

✓ Read Genesis 8:18-22 and discuss Noah's response to God's provision. How do you respond to God's provision in your life?

✓ What is your response to God's promise in these verses?

4. Abraham's call and journey to Canaan (Genesis 11:31—12:5). Abraham was called by God to become the father of a new people, a new nation chosen of God for the purpose of revealing his glory and goodness to the world! He was uprooted and reestablished in a new place. Ultimately, we would all be blessed because of this covenant promise to Abraham.

✓ Read Genesis 12:1-3 and compare it with Acts 3:25 and Galatians 3:16. How do you benefit from the promise made to Abraham almost four thousand years ago?

To link this history with the geography you learned last session, read Genesis 11:31—12:5 and review map 1 in session one, recalling the journey of Abraham to the Promised Land.

5. Joseph and slavery in Egypt (Genesis 37—50). The story of Joseph is one of God's grace in the midst of humanity's evil intent. Speaking to his brothers at their reunion together, Joseph says, "You intended to harm me, but God intended it for good to accomplish what is now being done, the saving of many lives" (Genesis 50:20).

✓ Joseph's story has great lessons for all of us. How is our character formed during long periods of disappointment, so that we can see God's ultimate purposes as Joseph did?

Three main themes of Christianity—creation, Fall, redemption—are uncovered in this early part of biblical history. Chuck Colson says of these three themes: "These categories provide the means to compare and contrast the various ideas and philosophies competing for allegiance in today's world, for they cover the central questions that any worldview must answer. Creation—Where did we come from and who are we? Fall—What has gone wrong with the world? Redemption—What can we do to fix it?" (*How Now Shall We Live*)

6. Moses and the exodus (Exodus 1—20). Moses was prepared for his crucial role through many tests. His leadership was indispensable for the beginning of a nation God had chosen for himself, but like us, Moses felt inadequate and insecure. Read Exodus 3:11 and feel your own doubts and fears. But then read God's response in 3:12. We have an "I will be with you" God.

✓ Describe how God has "been with you" recently in the midst of difficult challenges or overwhelming circumstances.

To help us understand his holiness and to keep us from the evil that can destroy us, God gave Moses the Ten Commandments as a guide for right and truthful living. Despite our sin, God gave us a plan for living in a fallen world.

Gaining a Foothold

These events are not fiction—they have become part of the history of God's work and his people. The book of Hebrews points to them as fact and as a place to find hope for our own lives. These early chapters of history provide the entire framework for the coming of Christ and the redemption of the world. Familiarize yourself with these events, for they form the backdrop for our faith today.

Trailmarkers

Often when we look at biblical history, we see "giants" of the faith. We have an inflated view of them and a weak view of what God can accomplish through us. Remember that God's great "Hall of Faith," as some call Hebrews 11, includes murderers, prostitutes, liars, adulterers and rebels. Yet they were used greatly despite their sin.

✓ Look at Acts 14:15 and James 5:17. What common theme is included here and how does that give you confidence?

Teamwork

Divide into teams and be creative! Use a little imagination and some artistic materials (if you have them on hand) to create a time line showing the major Old Testament events from this lesson. Draw a picture or symbol to describe each of the six events. List one word under each event that describes what that event means to you (such as, hope, courage, weakness, grace, friendship). Explain your drawings to the rest of the group.

Timeline

Creation	Fall	Flood	Abraham	Joseph	Moses

Reaching the Summit

How does our knowledge of the creation, Fall, flood and exodus affect us and our view of the world today?

Next Session

Based on what we learned about the spectacular birth of Israel at the time of the exodus, reflect on what you might expect to discover about the development of a new nation. Recall South Africa after apartheid, Germany after the Berlin Wall, America after the Revolutionary War or Russia after the breakup of the Soviet Union. What hopes did these people have? What fears and obstacles awaited them?

Close in Prayer

In all these events God was at work. Even when things looked dark, God always maintained a "trump card." Are there circumstances facing group members where the situation seems dark? Ask God to intervene and demonstrate his power and wisdom.

Session 3

Conquest, Kingdom, Captivity & Preparation

Discovering the importance of key events in Israel's history for the foundation of Christianity.

Establishing Base Camp

I was very deeply touched by the story of a coworker of mine. He was born in a repressive country and later relocated to the United States. When the Berlin Wall fell, friends in the United States helped Abel travel to Germany. In his bag he carried a hammer to strike a blow—for himself—at one of the monumental symbols of oppression. With tears in his eyes, he tells of the fragments he keeps at his house. Having spent my whole life in the United States, I will never fully comprehend what he will never forget.

The flow of history records the rise and fall of nations and empires. Session two included the fantastic story of God's power demonstrated in the creation of the world—followed by the tragic consequences of human failure and the burden of sin's impact on our world. But beginning with Noah and continuing with Abraham, God forged a new community of faith. Seventy of Abraham's descendants grew to become a nation of more than one million people during four hundred years of slavery in Egypt.

The spectacular demonstration of their rescue at the exodus turned bitter and disappointing. Those who saw God's power over the Egyptian armies failed to continue in faith. The result was forty years of life in the desert. We find Israel poised on the threshold of a new adventure in this session.

✔ Which members of your family tree have had the biggest impact on you and your siblings? How is that influence felt today?

✓ What events in your family history are causes for great joy? great sorrow or sadness?

Mapping the Trail

Predicting the future is risky business, but analyzing the past can provide answers to life's riddles we face each day. A nomadic way of life may suit the natural resources of the ancient Near East and much of the modern Middle East, but we are interested in learning how Israel adjusted to their new home as part of their faith journey with God! *Read Joshua 1:1-9.*

✓ As Israel enters the Promised Land, put yourself in their sandals and describe what expectations you have of God, your people and your future.

Beginning the Ascent

In session two we learned about the earliest history of the Old Testament leading up to the departure of more than one million people who formed the nation Israel from Egypt. Because they failed to trust in God as they first stood on the edge of their Promised Land, they lived in the desert wilderness of the Sinai Peninsula for forty years. Joshua led them across the Jordan River at the end of the forty years.

Following this momentous occasion, the history of Israel can be divided into four major eras:

1. Conquest and occupation—350 years
2. Development of the monarchy (kingdom)—120 years
3. Division and exile/captivity—350 years
4. Restoration and preparation—150 years

1. Conquest and occupation—350 years. Joshua was a military leader appointed by Moses and commissioned by God. When he died at the age of 110, many groups in Canaan had not been displaced (as God had commanded in Joshua 1:1-9) and much of the Promised Land was not occupied. The settlement of the rest of the Promised Land required repeated intervention by God. Israel did not obey and follow God's command to expel all the nations of Canaan (Deuteronomy 7:1-6). They sinned and turned from God and received the consequences of their sin, as Joshua had described (Joshua 23:9-13). God allowed Israel to be oppressed by others. But when they repented, he delivered them, using leaders called "judges" who lifted local oppression. The most famous of the judges are Gideon and Samson. As a result of the judges' military successes, Israel enjoyed long periods of peace.

Selected Judges	
Judge	*Oppressors*
Deborah	Canaanites
Gideon	Midianites
Jephthah	Ammonites
Samson	Philistines

2. Development of the monarchy (kingdom)—120 years. Moses anticipated the appointment of a king (Deuteronomy 17:14-20). The idea arose during the period of the judges but did not generate national interest until nearly four hundred years after the Israelites crossed the Jordan River. Israel rejected God as their king and sought a human king just as Moses predicted (1 Samuel 8:6-9).

The prophet Samuel anointed Saul as the first king of Israel. He came from the tribe of Benjamin. Saul failed the test of faith, and David, from the tribe of Judah, replaced him. David's son Solomon succeeded him. Each reigned for approximately forty years.

Early Kings of the Monarchy and Their Tribes
Saul (tribe of Benjamin) 1040 B.C. — 1010 B.C.
David (tribe of Judah) 1010 B.C. — 970 B.C.
Solomon (tribe of Judah) 970 B.C. — 931 B.C.

3. Division and exile/captivity—350 years. After a failed assassination plot and coup, Jeroboam of the tribe of Ephraim fled to Egypt. He returned after Solomon's death and tried to take the kingdom from Solomon's son, Rehoboam. Jealous of Rehoboam and eager for power, Jeroboam seceded with ten of the twelve tribes and established the northern kingdom. Rehoboam, leader of the remaining two tribes (Judah and Benjamin), became king of the southern kingdom. The result was two separate nations, Israel (ten northern tribes) and Judah (two southern tribes). See map 3 in session one for the boundaries of these kingdoms.

> "Few nations in the saga of man have experienced such a dynamic, turbulent, or influential history as the nation of Israel. Marred by tragedy—bathed in glory—loved by God—feared and despised by her neighbor nations: this is the story of Israel." (Leon Wood, *A Survey of Israel's History*)

As judgment for breaking God's covenant and worshiping false gods, God sent the Israelites into captivity. The northern kingdom, whose capital was Samaria, was destroyed by Assyria in 722 B.C. The southern kingdom of Judah fell to the Babylonians in 605 B.C.

Judah was the tribe through whom Messiah would come. Their rebellion was met by a seventy-year captivity (605-535 B.C.) as predicted by Jeremiah (Jeremiah 25). They turned from God and did not honor him by giving the land a sabbath rest every seventh year (as commanded in Leviticus 25:1-7). This disobedience occurred for 490 years, so God put them into captivity for seventy years—one year for every time Israel failed to observe the sabbath year.

4. Restoration and preparation—150 years. At the end of the monarchy, Jerusalem was repeatedly attacked between 625 B.C. and 586 B.C. Assyria to the north, Egypt to south and Babylon to the east competed for control of the ancient world.

Babylon won out and kept rulers on the throne in Jerusalem to provide a buffer in the region. The kings in Jerusalem continued to look for ways to overthrow Babylon's control. It all came to an end in 586 B.C. when Nebuchadnezzar of Babylon ordered his general to destroy the Jewish temple, burn the city and knock down the walls. The majority of the Jewish people were either killed or deported, leaving only a few poor farmers in the region.

After the seventy-year captivity ended, successive groups returned to their homeland.

1. Sheshbazzar, a descendant of Jehoiachin, led those who first returned to the devastated city with articles of gold and silver stolen from the temple by the Babylonians.

2. Zerubbabel, an early governor, began the work of rebuilding the temple, but the project was delayed for years due to local opposition and indifference on the part of the Jews.

3. The project was restarted through the ministry of two prophets, Haggai and Zechariah. The temple was finally completed in 516 B.C.

4. Later, Ezra returned to establish political and religious order on behalf on the Persian rulers in the same time frame as Nehemiah provided leadership necessary to rebuild Jerusalem's walls about 440 B.C.

Gaining a Foothold

The student of biblical history is not merely memorizing a set of facts to be recalled only for purposes of impressing (or irritating) others. These are the words and works of God from which we learn how he has graciously dealt with people through the ages. We learn that we, like Israel, deserve God's wrath but instead receive his blessing time and again. And we take comfort knowing God is involved in history; he is active and engaged. His redemptive work continues.

Trailmarkers

Below are some important passages listed for your reference. Do not try to read all of them at this time, but you might want to highlight them in your Bible when you are reviewing this material.

Among these passages, two are noteworthy and beneficial for memorization: Joshua 1:8-9 and 1 Samuel 16:7. Read these two verses and reflect on them together.

Passages Concerning Israel's History

Conquest and Occupation
Joshua 1:8-9: Joshua's commission.
Deuteronomy 11:22-23, 26-28: Blessings and curses for Israel as they enter the land.
Judges 21:25: The attitude and condition of Israel without a king.

Early Kingdom
1 Samuel 8:4-5: Israel asks for a king to replace God as their king.
1 Samuel 16:7: The kind of king God wanted—with David's heart.

Divided Kingdom and Captivity
1 Kings 11:11-13: God will break up Solomon's kingdom.
Jeremiah 25: God's people will go into captivity for seventy years.

Restoration and Preparation
Ezra 1—7: Rebuilding the Temple.
Nehemiah 1—6: Rebuilding the walls of Jerusalem.

Teamwork

Breathe a sigh of relief! This session contains a mountain of material, and it will take more study to master it. However, you can pick out some of the high points and remember them by doing the following.

Option one: Create several bookmarks. Using heavy paper or card stock, summarize selected Old Testament events with character names or triumphs and tragedy. Divide your group by four if you have enough members, and assign each one of the four eras. If your group is small, make one bookmark with Joshua and judges and another with selected kings. Compare your efforts, explaining why you included the information and pictures. Have a group member take the finished products to a copy center and reproduce the bookmark on heavy paper or card stock. Use the bookmarks in your Bible when you are reading the Old Testament to provide a simple reference.

Option two. Now that you have walked through the information about the four major periods, take a few minutes to quiz each other about them. Pair off and have each pair take a period of history and ask the rest of the group a question from that period. The others should try to answer the question without looking at the guide. Ask a question about a major event or key person of that period, and include a personal application in your question. You might even make it a contest or game. Keep the questions reasonable. Assign points based on whether members needed to consult their books or not. For example, here is a question about the monarchy period: Can you name in chronological order the three kings of the monarchy period and how many years each reigned? What did you understand about the human heart by observing these three kings?

Each team could ask one question of each of the other teams. Your leader can help you decide how to organize this exercise.

Reaching the Summit

God was at work throughout the Old Testament era as Israel's fortunes rose and fell. Identify two or three main lessons learned from this review of Israel's past. How do these values apply to our life in Christ?

Next Session

In the next session we will travel into the world of the New Testament and examine the life and ministry of Jesus Christ. For next time, flip through your Bible and compare the amount of material (pages or books) devoted to the New Testament (about one hundred years of history) versus the Old Testament (two thousand years). What does this tell you? Also look at the Gospel of John. How many chapters are devoted to the last week of Jesus' life compared with the rest of the book?

Close in Prayer

As you pray, reflect on a character whose story was noteworthy and ask God to make the lessons learned from him or her live in your heart as your face your own challenges each day.

Session 4

The Life of Christ

Getting a picture of Christ's life by following his footsteps.

 ### Establishing Base Camp

By most standards, my life is rich beyond measure. I had a safe, middle-class upbringing and a college education at a great school. I've been married for twenty-five years and have grown children who are establishing homes of their own. I've led a Boy Scout troop, served as a missionary overseas, pastored two churches and for over ten years worked for one of the most prestigious employers in the world (IBM). I am not bragging, just reflecting on all I have been privileged to experience.

But with all sincerity I must say that by far the biggest thrill I will ever have comes from realizing that the God of the universe walked on this earth and now lives in me. The wonder of it all is fresh with every heartbeat and passing breath! Jesus' life is in us now, and he has been living in believer's lives since the first century.

It is incredible to think that Jesus completed the work God gave him to do in just thirty-three years of life—and only three years of public ministry (John 17:3-4). He was focused and very passionate about his work and ministry. His call from God was clear, his mission focused and his resolve to complete the Father's will was unaltered. Our busy, complicated lives seem to draw more and more out of us each week. The result is we are left drained by an ever-increasing load of tasks that need our attention. Our mission gets cloudy, our passions run cool.

✔ What do you feel is the contribution God wants you to make in your family, job, community or church? Share it with the group. What would it take for you to accomplish this dream?

Mapping the Trail

✓ The Scriptures tend to focus on the ministry of Christ, giving very little detail of his childhood or early adult years. Why would the Gospels focus so much on Christ, particularly the last week of his life on earth?

✓ Discuss the highlights of Jesus' life. What were his defining moments?

✓ How would the average non-Christian person today answer the same question?

Beginning the Ascent

Jesus' public ministry begins with his baptism and forty-day wilderness temptation, and is completed in his final week of teaching, which culminated in his betrayal, crucifixion and resurrection.

Each of the Gospel writers had a different focus for writing. Matthew emphasized Christ as the messianic Jewish King, fulfilling the Old Testament prophecies. Luke wrote to Greeks and revealed Jesus as the Son of Man, a title denoting his deity. John organized his work around themes (like Jesus' "I am" statements and his many signs). Mark, probably the earliest Gospel written, is the most succinct, explaining Jesus as the Suffering Servant. For purposes of chronology, we will work with Mark's brief, focused account. You can read the other Gospels to get the full picture of Christ's ministry.

Phase one of Jesus' ministry: Preparation. In this part of his life, Jesus begins his public ministry. John the Baptist announces him as the promised Messiah. His baptism declares his commissioning by God the Father ("This is my beloved Son in whom I am well pleased!"), and his temptation in the wilderness provides spiritual strength.

> Jesus Christ is the central figure of the New Testament and focus of the Christian faith. The name indicates his role: Jesus, from the Hebrew *yeshua,* meaning "savior" or "Yahweh saves"; and Christ, from the Greek word for Messiah (*christos*), meaning "anointed one" (*Revell Bible Dictionary*).

Key Events

Announcement	Mark 1:1-8
Baptism	Mark 1:9-11
Temptation	Mark 1:12-13

✔ Discuss how the temptation of Christ (more fully described in Matthew 4:1-11) prepared him for his ministry. Why was this necessary?

Phase two of Jesus' ministry: Galilee region. This ministry lasted between two and two and a half years. It began just after Jesus' testing in the desert. At this point he calls the twelve apostles (Mark 3:14) and begins training them. His teaching (much of it in parables) and preaching (like the Sermon on the Mount) affect many people. His miracles of healing and power over nature testify that he is the Son of God. He also makes some short ministry tours outside the Galilee area during this time.

Jesus spent much of his time developing a core group of followers who could carry the gospel ministry into the world. The call to follow Jesus unfolded over a period of time. In John 1 his followers first became acquainted with him. Later in Matthew 4, Jesus asks them to leave their nets. Finally, he commissions all twelve as apostles (Mark 3:13-19).

✓ Of the twelve apostles who are you most familiar with?

✓ How many can you name?

1	5	9
2	6	10
3	7	11
4	8	12

Phase three of Jesus' ministry: Judea. The final six to nine months of Jesus' ministry were focused on deepening his relationships with the twelve apostles and preparing for the cross. He begins to reveal more about his impending death and resurrection (Mark 10:32-34). He begins in Jerusalem but also travels to Bethany, where he spends time with close friends Mary and Martha (and raises their brother Lazarus from the dead—John 11). Short trips to Jericho, where Zacchaeus the tax collector becomes a follower, and across the Jordan River are completed. Jesus then returns to Jerusalem for his final week.

Phase four of Jesus' ministry: Passion week and resurrection. Though only a week long, this part of Jesus' ministry is the focus of all of Scripture and thirty to forty percent of the Gospel writings. Selected events of the last week from the Gospel of Mark are provided in the box on page 38 for an overview.

✓ As you reflect on this last week of Jesus' life and public ministry, what thoughts come to mind about the fulfillment of his mission and the focus of his life? How does this impact you?

Day	Event	Scripture
Sunday	Triumphal entry into Jerusalem	Mark 11:1-11
Monday	Cleansing the temple	Mark 11:15-18
Tuesday	Temple teaching; anointed by Mary	Mark 12:35-37; 4:3-9
Wednesday(?)	Plot to kill Jesus	Mark 14:10-11
Thursday	Last Supper; prayer in the garden	Mark 14:12-42
Friday	Arrest (early morning), trials, crucifixion	Mark 14:43—15:46
Friday-Sunday	Death and burial	Mark 15:42-47
Sunday	Resurrection	Mark 16:1-8
Next 40 days	Resurrection appearances and ascension	Mark 16:9-20

[This timeline is adapted from *Chronological & Background Charts of the New Testament* by Wayne House, Zondervan, p. 103.]

✓ Look back again at map 4, "The Ministry of Jesus," for a sense of where some of the events we have discussed took place.

Gaining a Foothold

Linking the chronology sessions with the maps listed in session one will help you connect times and places. For example, look at map 4 (p. 17) and compare it to map 3 (p. 15). Try to imagine how Jesus felt as he walked past places like Jericho, where Jews first entered the Promised Land fifteen hundred years earlier! What were his thoughts as he entered Jerusalem, capital of the southern kingdom destroyed in 586 B.C.? When he met the woman at the well at Sychar in Samaria, just outside Shechem, did he envision Assyria destroying the northern kingdom in 722 B.C.?

Trailmarkers

Here are four key verses that reveal the identity and mission of Jesus. Try to commit one or more to memory.

Scripture	Identity	Purpose
Matthew 16:16	Messiah	Announce God's kingdom
Mark 10:45	Suffering Servant	Give his life for us
Luke 19:10	Son of Man	Seek and save the lost
John 20:31	Son of God	Call us to believe in him

Teamwork

Option one: You are a newspaper reporter in A.D. 60 and arrive in Jerusalem. You have heard of Jesus and have interviewed people about his life and ministry. The *Galilee Gazette* has asked you for a brief survey of his ministry, but they only have two paragraphs (about a half-page) of space in this Sunday's edition for your work. Write a brief, focused description of Jesus' ministry, including a few key events. You may be creative with this, but stick to the Bible facts!

Option two: Using old magazines and markers, draw a "picture" of the ministry of Christ as you now understand it. The picture could be a collage, or it could be a timeline with graphics. When you have finished, show your work to the group and explain why you chose to portray his life that way.

Reaching the Summit

Jesus devoted most of his time to his closest friends. How do Jesus' ministry choices affect us today?

Next Session

Paul and Peter were foundational to the spread of Christianity in the early church. Read Acts 1:1-11 and reflect on Jesus' purpose for the church and how the gospel was to be communicated. How are we doing today with Jesus' commission in Acts 1?

Close in Prayer

Reflect on the life of Jesus as you pray. Through the testimony of Jesus' life, let the Holy Spirit teach you or challenge you to greater devotion.

Session 5

The Church

Understanding the birth and growth of the church.

 ### Establishing Base Camp

I've had the opportunity and privilege to worship and teach in churches large and small across the United States and Europe. When I joined the corporate world at IBM, the interviewing manager asked how I would like being a little fish in a big pond, compared to where I was before. More than a decade later, I know the answer. No matter how much I have sold, how many awards I might receive, how many trips I have taken or how many promotions and raises may come my way, my heart beats fastest for the church.

When I meet with a group of people to learn more about Jesus Christ and how to follow him, my heart beats fast. My heart races with joy when I meet with others to worship the God who made me. And it pulses with life when I am on my knees praying with others for the work God is doing around the world. It just doesn't get any better than this!

The church is the bride of Christ and the hope of the world. Where would so many of us be without the church? Because of this "new community" that was created at Pentecost and continues to express the new covenant in Christ, we have life and hope! Unfortunately not everyone has a life-giving church experience to look back on. Some churches get off mission, others excel in one or two areas of ministry but seem to neglect others. Others have drifted so far that they have abandoned the foundational truths of the faith. But many churches are places where people meet Christ and build significant relationships with others mature in the faith. Church is a place where we discover our spiritual gifts and begin doing ministry, where we learn the Word of God and find grace when sin takes us off track.

✓ What role did the church play in your life as you were growing up? What excited you about the church? What frustrated you? If you had no church experience growing up, talk about your impression of the church in your early years.

Mapping the Trail

The church was "born" at Pentecost in the early 30s A.D. in the city of Jerusalem. The outpouring of the Holy Spirit in Acts 2:1-13 was clear evidence that God was doing something new that would change the world. Peter's sermon (Acts 2:14-40) clearly made a case for Jesus as Messiah and called all listeners to repentance.

✓ Read Acts 2:41-47 and describe the characteristics of that first church. What makes a church become so life-giving?

Beginning the Ascent

The book of Acts was written by Luke to show what Jesus continued to do through his followers after he was taken into heaven (Acts 1:4). It is a book about the Holy Spirit's work to launch the church and infuse it with power to transform the hearts and lives of people around the world.

The primary characters in Acts 1—7 are Peter and John, with Stephen becoming the first martyr in the church. In Acts 8—12, Peter, John, James and Philip take center stage. Their ministry activity (at least the parts described in the New Testament) was limited to the regions of Judea and Samaria.

Paul was dramatically converted as he was persecuting believers (Acts 9). Barnabas introduced him to the other disciples (Acts 9:27) and recruited him to help establish a church in Antioch (in Syria).

✔ How did you come to faith in Christ? How did you get connected to your first church? Who helped or guided you in each of these decisions?

Paul's journeys to the north and west of Palestine created opportunities to plant and strengthen churches throughout Asia Minor and Greece. Acts 13—28 details the ministry efforts of Paul and others as churches grew and were established. Here are highlights of the three missionary journeys of Paul.

First journey: Paul and Barnabas left Antioch and sailed for Cyprus, then on to Asia Minor (modern-day Turkey). They visited at least seven cities en route where they taught about Jesus and established congregations of believers (Acts 13—14). At the end of twelve months of travel they returned to their home base of Antioch in Syria, about 350 miles north of Jerusalem. Paul probably wrote Galatians during this journey.

Second journey: Paul and Barnabas parted company (Acts 15). Paul traveled overland from Antioch to Asia Minor, visiting the churches he established the previous year. As he reached the western shore, a vision (Acts 16:8-9) prompted him to cross to Macedonia (northern Greece). He taught in cities like Philippi, Thessalonica, Athens and Corinth. The journey lasted nearly two years, with Paul returning to Antioch once more. Paul most likely wrote 1 and 2 Thessalonians during the second journey.

Third journey: Paul traveled to Ephesus and began a lengthy ministry from that city, traveling back and forth to cities in Greece. During this period he wrote letters to the churches in Corinth and Rome. Paul concluded this journey by traveling to Jerusalem for a festival.

✔ Have you ever been part of a new church start-up? If so, explain what it was like. If not, describe what you think it might be like to be part of a new church. What are the obstacles and challenges? What are the benefits or blessings you might anticipate? What makes a new church thrive?

Later years: Paul was arrested in Jerusalem by some Jews and later imprisoned by the Romans to protect him from mob action. Paul's citizenship enabled him to appeal to the emperor, necessitating a long voyage to Rome. At the end of the book of Acts, Paul endures two years of house arrest, awaiting trial. This is his first Roman imprisonment, a period during which he wrote letters to Philemon and to churches in Colossae, Ephesus and Philippi. Known as the Prison Epistles, these letters bring us clarity about the person of Christ and the nature of the church, the new community.

According to the best sources, Paul was released in A.D. 62 and traveled to Macedonia in 64 (Greece), where he was arrested again and taken to Rome. Peter was likely in Rome the same time and wrote 1 and 2 Peter in A.D. 63-64. The final stage of Paul's life ends with his death in Rome. While awaiting execution, he wrote letters to his close friends and ministry partners Titus and Timothy. Peter was also martyred in A.D. 64.

Little is know of the rest of the New Testament era except for glimpses contained in later letters by John. The New Testament, and the Bible, concludes with a vision of God's triumph in the "Revelation of Jesus Christ." John spent most of his later years in exile on the island of Patmos, just off the cost of Asia Minor.

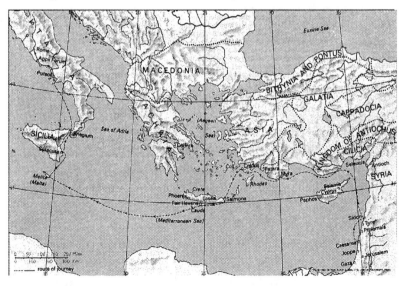

Map 6. Paul's journey to Rome

Peter, Paul, John and many New Testament believers followed their callings to the end. They sacrificed much for the church and the spread of the gospel.

✔ How does it make you feel when you think that God might call you to a fate similar to that of the apostles?

✔ What do you think the reward is for those who follow Christ wherever he calls?

Trailmarkers

Here are some verses about the life and development of the church. Read through them and choose one to commit to memory. Reflect on what it says about the church or how the people of God should reflect Christ in the church.

"I tell you that you are Peter, and on this rock I will build my church, and the gates of Hades will not overcome it" (Matthew 16:18).

"They devoted themselves to the apostles' teaching and to the fellowship, to the breaking of bread and to prayer" (Acts 2:42).

"Then the church throughout Judea, Galilee and Samaria enjoyed a time of peace. It was strengthened; and encouraged by the Holy Spirit, it grew in numbers, living in the fear of the Lord" (Acts 9:31).

"Now to him who is able to do immeasurably more than all we ask or imagine, according to his power that is at work within us, to him be glory in the church and in Christ Jesus throughout all generations, for ever and ever! Amen" (Ephesians 3:20).

Gaining a Foothold

There are three main images of the church described in Scripture: the body of Christ, the family of God and God's holy temple. In the body we each have a function that gives the body life and purpose, and Christ is our head who sustains, protects and provides for the church. As a family we are brothers and sisters in Christ and share true community. As a temple, we are home to the Holy Spirit, and we are building blocks to construct a church which glorifies God with purity and passion.

Teamwork

Read Ephesians 4:1-16 together and list the characteristics of a vibrant church. You might want to divide your group into two. Team one could take verses 1-8 and team two could read verses 11-16. This is the kind of church that Christ dreamed of and the apostles and other disciples labored to build. It is a "prevailing church" against which the gates of hell have no chance!

"As individual members of the body of Christ, believers are the key players in the unfolding in the most important of all the stories that compete for headlines on the front page of history." (Gilbert Bilezikian, *Christianity 101*)

Marks of a Prevailing Church

1

2

3

4

5

Reaching the Summit

As you celebrate the church, discuss what aspects of today's church you find most effective. Where do we all need to put more effort?

Next Session

Next time, we will try to bring together what you have learned over the last five sessions. Wrapping up this study will be the beginning, not the end, of your experience with the world of the Bible. Ask God to help you recall what you learned so that your understanding of his Word increases. As the Bible comes to life in your mind, ask God to help you follow his leading more closely than ever before.

Close in Prayer

Pray for wisdom about your role in the life of the church and how you can spread the ministry that is so richly described in the New Testament. Focus on group needs as well, and encourage members to "be the church" to one another, caring for and praying for each other.

Session 6

Putting It All Together

Getting an overview of the chronology and geography of the Bible.

Establishing Base Camp

The time span from Abraham to the beginning of the church covered a period of more than two thousand years. The Bible was written by close to forty authors who lived and traveled through the ancient world. Every single event contributes to the overall picture and leads us to our place in world history. Sometimes this makes us feel small and insignificant. But if we look deeper at the biblical story, it is a tale of God's extraordinary work through ordinary people who are available and willing to work with him.

✓ Reflect for a few minutes on your own place in the history of faith and God's interaction with human beings. What events in the Bible would you single out as leading to your experience with God through Jesus Christ?

✓ What event or story has had the most impact on your life?

Mapping the Trail

In this session we are going to look at the Old and New Testament "Halls of Faith." Men and women from history were used greatly by God despite their sin and weakness, allowing his glory to shine through them. As you look at these people, place them in their chronological and geographical setting, based on what we have learned. Use your maps and notes from previous sessions to help.

✓ How might our personal statistics (age, gender and so on) and role in the community around us tend to affect our interpretation of history?

✓ How might we view events from this perspective and yet avoid the errors of misinformation and oversimplification?

Teamwork

Here is where we pull it all together so you can get a grasp of the great amount of information you have your hands on. Keep track of the time, devoting thirty minutes to the New Testament and thirty minutes to the Old Testament sections. Work together as a team. Everyone does not have to complete the entire chart. Pair up to work on various people and events. Skim the Bible passages listed if you are need some help.

First, look over the charts. We will give you more than one option on how to fill them out. Your leader will have some ideas as well. The "Old Testament Hall of Faith" table lists people of faith from Hebrews 11. The writer of Hebrews wanted the church to know that although they were facing difficulties and persecution, we can look to the men and women who went before us. They too faced various trials but exercised faith in a big God.

Old Testament Hall of Faith

Name	Location	Date/Time	Significance	Text
Abel & Cain				Genesis 4
Noah				Genesis 7—9
Abraham (1)				Genesis 12
Abraham (2)				Genesis 17
Abraham (3)				Genesis 22
Isaac				Genesis 27
Jacob				Genesis 49
Joseph				Genesis 50
Moses				Exodus 2
Joshua				Exodus 14
Rahab				Joshua 6
Samson				Judges 13—16
David				1 Samuel 17
Samuel				1 Samuel 3

The "New Testament Hall of Faith" table lists New Testament men and women whose life of faith we hold as examples. Their exploits range across the New Testament and thus occupy a wide band of both time and place. These key figures of the New Testament era were instrumental in bringing the message of redemption to the world.

The New Testament Hall of Faith

Name	Location	Date/Time	Significance	Text
Joseph & Mary (1)				Luke 2:1-7
Joseph & Mary (2)				Matthew 2:13-15
John the Baptist				Mark 1:4-8
Jesus (1)				Mark 1:9-13
Jesus (2)				Matthew 4:23-25
Jesus (3)				John 12:12-16
Peter (1)				Matthew 14:22-34
Peter (2)				Acts 2:14-41
Stephen				Acts 7
Paul (1)				Acts 9:1-6
Barnabas				Acts 11:19-26
Paul (2)				Acts 13:1-5
Paul (3)				Acts 16:6-12
John				Revelation 1:9-11

Option one: Break into two groups and have one fill in the Old Testament chart and the other fill in the New Testament chart. Give each group thirty to forty minutes to complete the charts together. Then ask one representative from each group to use their chart as a guide and "talk through the history" of the Old or New Testament, whichever they worked on.

Option two: Have a group member draw a simple map of the Near Eastern world (like map 5 on page 18, or a larger version of the map below). Draw it on a large sheet of paper, the size of a tabletop game board—two feet by three feet. Divide the group into teams of two or three. Have the teams read the passages describing the exploit(s) of the biblical character on the charts and create a small marker or pictogram for each, placing the markers on the map. Each marker should include approximate time frame and place names. Markers can be made from

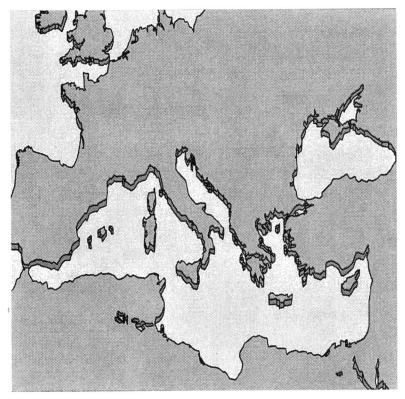

blank 3 × 5 cards or by drawing on the map. When you are done, you'll have a map with major historical events and figures, giving you a visual framework of the chronology and geography of the Bible.

Reaching the Summit

The Bible contains a selected history of God's interaction with the world he created and the creatures he made to live in it. It is rich with stories of God's love for people who matter to him. It is rich with the stories of the real-life success and failures of people who seek to live for God or escape from him.

Reading the Bible in bite-sized chunks over a long time will fill hearts with courage, inflame imaginations with dreams of adventures for God and give people a sense of the rich heritage that comes from belonging to the people of God.

Next Session

Choose your next study topic together. Make plans to include regular Bible reading in your group meetings so that you will get to know God better.

Close in Prayer

Thank God that men and women throughout the history of the human race have found ways to follow him. Their life situation was sometimes very challenging, presenting obstacles, but their faith still triumphed.

Ask God to make you a person who climbs over his or her surroundings and is not defeated by them. Ask God to help you discover the role he wants you to play in the history of his people.

Leader's Notes

Few ventures are more defining than leading a group that produces changed lives and sharper minds for the cause of Christ. At Willow Creek we have seen small groups transform our church, offer deeper levels of biblical community and provide an environment where truth can be understood and discussed with enthusiasm. So we have focused on a group-based study rather than a classroom-lecture format or individual study (though these studies can profitably be used in both settings with minor adaptations).

Each method of learning has its strengths; each has its weaknesses. In personal study one can spend as little or as much time as desired on an issue and can focus specifically on personal needs and goals. The downside: there is no accountability to others, no one to challenge thoughts or assumptions, no one to provide support when life comes tumbling down around you. The classroom is ideal for proclaiming truth to many at one time and for having questions answered by those with expertise or knowledge in a subject area. But the pace of the class depends largely on the teacher, and there is limited time to engage in the discussion of personal issues. The small group is optimal for life-on-life encouragement, prayer and challenge. And it provides a place where learning is enhanced through the disciplines of biblical community. But small groups are usually not taught by content experts and cannot focus solely on one person's needs.

Our hope is that you will be able to use this curriculum in a way that draws from the best of all three methods. Using the small group as a central gathering place, personal preparation and study will allow you to focus on your own learning and growth goals. The small group activity will provide you with an engaging environment for refining your understanding and gaining perspective into the lives and needs of others. And perhaps by inviting a knowledgeable outsider to the group (or a cluster of small groups at a Saturday seminar, for example) you could gain the benefits of solid teaching in a given subject area. In any case your devotion to

Christ, your commitment to your local church and your obedience to the Word of God are of utmost importance to us. Our desire is to see you "grow in the grace and knowledge of the Lord Jesus Christ."

Leadership Tips

Here are some basic guidelines for leaders. For more extensive leadership support and training we recommend that you consult *The Willow Creek Guide to Leading Lifechanging Small Groups,* where you will find many suggestions for leading creative groups.

Using the leader's notes. The questions in the study will not be repeated in the leader's notes. Instead, we have provided comments, clarifications, additional information, leadership tips or group exercises. These will help you guide the discussion and keep the meeting on track.

Shared leadership. When leading a small group remember that your role is to guide the discussion and help draw people into the group process. Don't try to be the expert for everything. Seek to involve others in the leadership process and activities of group life (hosting meetings, leading prayer, serving one another, leading parts of the discussion and so forth).

Preparation. Your work between meetings will determine group effectiveness during meetings. Faithful preparation does not mean that you will control the meeting or that it will move exactly as you planned. Rather, it provides you with a guiding sense of the desired outcomes of the time together so that you can gauge the pace of the meeting and make adjustments along the way. Above all, make sure you are clear about the overall goal of the meeting. Then even if you get appropriately sidetracked dealing with a personal concern or a discussion of related issues, you can graciously help the group refocus on the goal of the meeting. Also, preparation will allow you to observe how others are engaging with the material. *You should complete the study* before coming to the meeting. You can participate in the group activities at the meeting, but take time to become personally acquainted with the material in case you need to alter the schedule or amount of time on each section.

Purpose. The series is designed to help people understand the Word and be confident in their ability to read, study and live its lifechanging truths. Bible 101 is not designed for a group whose primary goal is caregiving or support. That does not mean you will avoid caring for each other, praying for needs or supporting one another through personal crises. It simply means that the *entire* focus of the group is not for these purposes. At the same time, the content should never take precedence over the process of transformation. There will be appropriate times to set the curriculum aside and pray. Or you may want to spend an evening having fun together. Remember, Jesus did not say, "Go therefore into all the world and complete the curriculum." Our focus is to make disciples. The curriculum is a tool, not a master. Use it consistently and with discernment, and your group will be well-served. But be clear about the primary focus of the group as you gather, and remind people every few weeks about the core purpose so that the group does not drift. So even though this is designed for six meetings per study guide, you might take longer if you have a meeting that focuses entirely on prayer or service.

Length of Meeting. We assume that you have about seventy to ninety minutes for this meeting, including prayer and some social time. If you have more or less time, adjust accordingly, especially if you have a task-based group. In that case, since you must complete the task (working on a ministry team or serving your church in some way), you will have to be selective in what you cover unless you can devote at least one hour to the meeting. In the format described below, feel free to play with the time allowed for "Beginning the Ascent," "Trailmarkers" and "Teamwork." We have given general guidelines for time to spend on each section. But depending on the size of group (we recommend about eight members), familiarity with the Bible and other group dynamics, you will have to make adjustments. After a few meetings you should have a good idea of what it will take to accomplish your goals.

Format. We have provided you with a general format. But feel free to provide some creativity or a fresh approach. You can begin with prayer, for example, or skip the "Establishing Base Camp" group opener and dive right into the study. We recommend that you follow the format closely early in the group process. As your group and your leadership skills mature and progress, you should feel increasing freedom to bring your creativity and experience to the meeting format. Here is the framework for the format in each of the guides in this series.

 Establishing Base Camp

This orients people to the theme of the meeting and usually involves a group opener or icebreaker. Though not always directly related to the content, it will move people toward the direction for the session. A base camp is the starting point for any mountain journey.

 Mapping the Trail

In this component we get clear about where we will go during the meeting. It provides an overview without giving away too much and removing curiosity.

 Beginning the Ascent

This is the main portion of the meeting: the climb toward the goal. It is the teaching and discussion portion of the meeting. Here you will find questions and explanatory notes. You will usually find the following two components included.

Pullouts. These provide additional detail, clarification or insight into content or questions that may arise in the participants' minds during the session.

Charts/Maps. Visual learners need more than words on a page. Charts, maps and other visuals combined with the content provide a brief, concise summary of the information and how it relates.

Gaining a Foothold

Along the trail, people can drift off course or slip up in their understanding. These footholds are provided for bringing them into focus on core issues and content.

 Trailmarkers

These are key biblical passages or concepts that guide our journey. Participants will be encouraged to memorize or reflect on them for personal growth and for the central biblical basis behind the teaching.

 Teamwork

This is a group project, task or activity that builds a sense of community and shared understanding. It will be different for each study guide and for each lesson, depending on the author's design and the purpose of the content covered.

 Reaching the Summit

This is the end of the content discussion, allowing members to look back on what they have learned and capture it in a brief statement or idea. This "view from the top" will help them once again focus on the big picture after spending some time on the details.

Balancing caregiving and study/discussion. One of the most difficult things to do in a group, as I alluded to above, is balancing the tension between providing pastoral and mutual care to members and getting through the material. I have been in small groups where needs were ignored to get the work done, and I have been in groups where personal needs were the driving force of the group to the degree that the truth of the Word was rarely discussed. These guides are unique because they are designed to train and teach processes that must take place in order to achieve its purpose. But the group would fail miserably if someone came to a meeting and said, "I was laid off today from my job," and the group said a two-minute prayer and then opened their curriculum. So what do you do? Here are some guidelines.

1. People are the most important component of the group. They have real needs. Communicate your love and concern for people even if they don't always get all the work done or they get sidetracked.

2. When people disclose hurts or problems, address each disclosure with empathy and prayer. If you think more time should be devoted to someone, set aside time at the end of the meeting, inviting members to stay for additional prayer or to console the person. Cut the meeting short by ten minutes to accomplish this. Or deal with it right away for ten to fifteen minutes, take a short break, then head into the study.

3. Follow up with people. Even if you can't devote large portions of the meeting time to caregiving, you and others from the group can provide this between meetings over the phone or in other settings. Also learn to leverage your time. For example, if your meeting begins at 7:00 p.m., ask the member in need and perhaps one or two others from the group to come at 6:30 p.m. for sharing and prayer. A person will feel loved, your group will share in the caregiving, and it is not another evening out for people.

4. Assign prayer partners or groups of three to be little communities within the group. Over the phone or in occasional meetings outside the group (before church and so on) they could connect and check in on how life is going.

5. For serious situations, solicit help from others, including pastors or other staff at church. Do not go it alone. Set boundaries for people with serious care needs, letting them know that the group can devote some but not substantial meeting time to support them. "We all know that Dave is burdened by his son's recent illness, so I'd like to spend the first ten minutes tonight to lift him up in prayer and commit to support Dave through this season. Then, after our meeting I'd like us to discuss any specific needs you (Dave) might have over the next two to three weeks (such as meals, help with house chores, etc.) and do what we can to help you meet those needs." Something to that effect can keep the group on track but still provide a place to express compassion.

Take time to look at the entire series if you have chosen only one of the guides. Though each can be used as a stand-alone study, there is much to benefit from in the other guides because each covers material essential for a complete overview of how to study and understand the Bible. We designed the guides in series form so that you can complete them in about a year if you meet weekly, even if you take a week off after finishing each guide.

A Word About Leadership

One of your key functions as a small group leader is to be a cheerleader—someone who seeks out signs of spiritual progress in others and makes some noise about it. What have you seen God doing in your group members' lives as a result of this study? Don't assume they've seen that progress—and definitely don't assume they are beyond needing simple words of encouragement. Find ways to point out to people the growth you've seen. Let them know it's happening, and that it's noticeable to you and others.

There aren't a whole lot of places in this world where people's spiritual progress is going to be recognized and celebrated. After all, wouldn't you like to hear someone say something like that to you? Your group members feel the same way. You have the power to make a profound impact through a sincere, insightful remark.

Be aware also that some groups get sidetracked by a difficult member or situation that hasn't been confronted. And some individuals could be making significant progress, but they just need a nudge. "Encouragement" is not about just saying "nice" things; it's about offering *words that urge*. It's about giving courage (en-*courage*-ment) to those who lack it.

So leaders, take a risk. Say what needs to be said to encourage your members as they grow in their knowledge of the Bible. Help them not just amass more information, but move toward the goal of becoming fully devoted followers of Jesus Christ. Go ahead; make their day!

Session 1. Geography of the Bible.
Introduce the Session (1 min.) Go over the purpose and goal.

Purpose: This session is designed to explain the basic features of the biblical world. A sense of the natural world will make the Bible narratives come to life. Applying biblical truths will become easier when participants can put the characters in the appropriate setting.

Goal: Be able to identify, locate and describe the places (land areas, major bodies of water, geographic features) where major biblical events took place and understand how the settings impact those events.

While geography may not be everyone's favorite subject, the biblical world is much more than an endless desert. Our mental picture of it is drawn from stories we may have heard repeatedly such as "wandering in the wilderness," David and Goliath (open, rural battlefield), and Daniel in the lion's den (a combination royal zoo and torture chamber).

Help group members realize that learning a little geography will enrich Bible reading. Suggest that group members take a few minutes to use their imagination each time they approach the Word to keep it in perspective.

The land of the Bible is not simply an arid region or a windswept desert. It is a tropical climate, not temperate or equatorial. It is a land of diversity and beauty, qualities that shape the stories of the Old Testament.

Establishing Base Camp (10 min.) Read through this and help people get a sense of the size of the Holy Land and the surrounding area. Encourage one or two people to answer the questions at the end.

Unless you have recently lived in a developing region, it can be hard to envision what life is like without modern inventions. For example, if I wanted to help someone get from my house to downtown Chicago and the lakefront or Sears Tower without jumping in the car and getting on the expressway, I would need to provide additional information. Such information would include:

• the *direction* to travel

....

- *length* of time in hours, days or weeks
- *milestones* or *stopping points* along the way
- *resources* needed for the journey (food, money, clothes)
- *barriers* and *dangers* (rivers, mountains, ravines, robbers)

▨ **Mapping the Trail (10 min.)** Refer to map 1 as you read this together. The objective here is to get familiar with the general landscape and terrain, both on the map and visually. Help group members catch the rich scenes in the Bible. Our crowded, cosmopolitan urban settings have much in common with the cities of the Bible. Beyond the cities, rural scenes and quiet-paced lives were also typical.

👞 **Beginning the Ascent (30 min.)** Help the group move through the maps and through the descriptions of the natural and human-made features of the area.

Cities were situated on mountains and high places for protection and for navigation. The higher you are, the better to spot an enemy or chart a travel route through difficult terrain. Obviously, water is essential to life—for drinking, feeding livestock and watering crops.

Old Testament places to know. Encourage group members as you work together to locate all of these places. Most are located on map 1, but the Jordan River and Dead Sea are easier to find on map 2.

Some of the major urban centers of the Old Testament are Mesopotamia (Ur, Babylon, Nineveh and Harran), the Holy Land (Shechem, Bethel, Mamre/Hebron, Jericho, Jerusalem), and Egypt (Memphis, near the Nile Delta and Thebes, several hundred miles upstream).

On map 3 you can see that Shechem and Jerusalem were the respective capitals of the northern and southern kingdoms. Later, Samaria (not on map 3 but just northwest of Shechem) became the capital of the northern kingdom. As you trace the boundaries of the divided kingdom, notice that a great enemy of God's people, the Philistines, are located along the shore. David had many battles with them, including one with a giant named Goliath.

New Testament places to know. The sites of Jesus' ministry can be found on maps 4 and 5. Take a few moments to look at map 4 and see some of Jesus' significant ministry moments. You might want to become familiar with a few of these as you prepare for the meeting. Focus particularly on Jesus' birthplace, first miracle, feeding the five thousand and crucifixion.

Note also how his ministry is divided primarily between the Galilean region in the north and the Judean region in the south. Samaria, the home of a people the Jews despised (see Luke 9:52-53 and John 4), separates these two regions. Foreigners had been relocated in the region after Assyria deported the Jews of the northern kingdom into captivity when the capital Samaria fell in 722 B.C. Assyrians brought

Jewish priests in to teach them how to worship, but they also served their own gods. Consequently, Jews viewed them as idolaters and unworthy inhabitants of the land.

On map 5 simply help your group get the overall scope of Paul's work and the spread of the church. Show how the gospel moved from Jerusalem all the way to Rome and beyond. Help them get a greater appreciation for the spread of the church in only about thirty to forty years time after the resurrection. Given the slow travel methods, Paul's arrests and imprisonment, and difficult church problems, it is a miracle that so much happened so soon.

For your information, here's some interesting and helpful material in case you need it. Do not cover this with the group unless it provides insight into a relevant question or problem.

1. Coastal plains/fertile valley/cultivated fields. Numbers 13:23-30 describes a land flowing with milk and honey, evidenced by grape clusters that could be carried on a pole between two men. This did not come about by accident, especially in an area now quite barren; what the Israelites found was no doubt the result of skillful agricultural development.

2. Once forested hills and mountains. In Joshua 17:15-18 the land allotted to this tribe did not appear to be enough to support them and their flocks; they didn't want to be hunting sheep and goats in the forests. Joshua told them there was enough forested land to support them for quite a while, as long as they were willing to clear it for pasture.

The temple Solomon had built in 1 Kings 7:2 had a length of nearly 150 feet, but the surprising part is that the roof had a span of 75 feet and a height of 45 feet. To support a roof that wide and high required a plentiful and robust supply of cedar forests.

3. Jordan Valley. The source of the Jordan lies twenty-five miles north of the Sea of Galilee, more than one thousand feet about sea level in the modern-day Golan Heights. By the time the Jordan reaches the Sea of Galilee, it drops to 682 feet *below* sea level. Galilee is itself twelve miles long. When the river leaves the Sea of Galilee, it travels sixty-five more miles before it empties into the Dead Sea, dropping through many dangerous rapids to its final depth of 1292 feet below sea level.

4. Barren wilderness regions. In Deuteronomy 1:19 Moses led the Israelites through desert regions for forty years before entering the Promised Land.

In Genesis 21:30 Abraham pitched his tent near a large tree but still had to dig wells to find water.

5. Towns, villages and urban centers.

Ur: See Genesis 11:27-30. Ur was the leading city of that era and Abraham's home from his birth.

Jericho: An early example of a walled city in Canaan. The Israelites had been living as nomads in tents for nearly forty years; imagine a generation of refugees today who set out on foot to capture a modern city. How would they begin to approach the task? The prospect of attacking fortified cities had frightened the previous generation. Compare the story of reconnaissance in the Promised Land (Numbers 13:28-29).

Jerusalem: David captured this Jebusite citadel on Mt. Zion and made it his fortress and royal residence. It became the Holy City (2 Samuel 5:7).

Nineveh: This city was Jonah's destination, home for more than 120,000 people. Much larger than Jericho, Jonah could *not* walk around it seven times in a single day. It took him three days to walk through the city (Jonah 3:3; 4:11).

Trailmarkers (10 min.) Read these three passages to show the significance of geography in the Bible. Challenge group members to memorize Acts 1:8 together or on their own.

Teamwork (15 min.) The Acts 7 passage is a great geographical and chronological overview of Israel's history. Using subgroups will allow people to work in teams and yet give them all a chance to participate. Simply ask the readers to read the passage, stopping only to allow members to locate places on the maps. It is a long passage, so there is no time for commentary; focus on the geography first. Then you can discuss the question.

Note that Midian (the desert area east of the Red Sea), in Acts 7:29, is not listed on map 1. Neither is Mt. Sinai, partly because no one knows exactly where it is. It would be located somewhere on the southern end of the Sinai Peninsula, which is the area between the forks of the Red Sea on map 1. Also the temple in 7:46-47 is located in Jerusalem, though the city is not mentioned in the passage.

Stephen spends time giving this history because he has been accused of breaking the Old Testament law and defiling the temple (Acts 6:13-14), so he traces the history of redemption starting with the father of the Jews (Abraham). Stephen tries to show them that Israel has often rejected God's messengers, the prophets, and is now rejecting his greatest messenger, Jesus Christ, who fulfills the law of Moses (verse 37). At this statement they end his story by stoning him.

Reaching the Summit (5 min.) This session has covered a lot of material. Assure the group that this geographical background information will become the framework into which we pour the chronology of the Bible. The story of God's redemptive plan involves people as well as places and events. Our lives too are the result of God's work through people in various times and places. These become defining moments in our own redemptive stories.

Next Session (10 min.) This exercise will prepare people to think in biblical terms about chronology. Chronology is not merely a set of dates. Rather, it is the story of significant events that outline the great plan and activity of God. Not all the details are given, just the major points.

Close in Prayer (10 min.) Pray that God will meet your people this week in powerful ways. Pray for any needs expressed.

Session 2. Creation to Law.
Introduce the Session (1 min.) Go over the purpose and goal.

Purpose: The purpose of this session is to gain a familiarity with selected important historical events in biblical history during the earliest recorded period.

Goal: The goal is to identify six major events in early Old Testament history (and some of the persons involved) and understand the significant impact of these events in God's redemptive plan and in your life today.

This session is the first of four lessons that cover the panorama of biblical history, a tall order. Keep things moving and focus on the selected events as much as possible. Spanning thousands of years of history in four meetings limits our scope and the depth of coverage. Nevertheless, there is plenty of meat here for the serious member and yet it should be accessible to newer Christians as well.

It has been said that if we don't learn from history, we are doomed to repeat it. God's character and power are revealed in the history of the human race. And his redemptive plan unfolds on the pages of Scripture from Genesis to Revelation.

 Establishing Base Camp (10 min.) The purpose for talking about family history is to see how events and experiences—positive and negative—shape who we are. It is also designed to help people focus on the major events because that is what the Bible does. The Bible does not give all the details of every event, and certainly the writers (inspired by the Holy Spirit) have selected only certain significant events. Asking people to do the same thing when describing their own family history helps them understand the purpose of history in the Bible. Selected events are chosen to provide the reader with the history of God's work of redemption. Sometimes this requires that many details are covered and at other times an overview is sufficient.

Mapping the Trail (10 min.) This question has two purposes: (1) to see how much of the early Bible history your members already know, and (2) to see what stories in the Bible are their favorites. This gives you a chance to understand their interests. A follow-up question to some members could be, How has that story been meaningful to you over the years? This gives you a chance to get to know each other a little better.

Beginning the Ascent (30 min.) The six major events provide a framework for the entire Bible. As you work through these with your group, answer the questions or do the exercises suggested.

1. Creation. This is a fairly straightforward exercise, but sometimes groups can get off track debating the age of the earth or whether the days of creation are literal days or represent periods of history, thus requiring many years for creation. This is not the time or place to discuss these. Encourage members who have questions here to consult books on the subject or a Bible dictionary or encyclopedia.

2. Fall. Consequences for sin are sometimes far-reaching. Discuss these with the group. Only three consequences are asked for, but there are a number of possible responses.

☐ The serpent was cursed. He would eat dust (the symbol of death, *NIV Study Bible*) and crawl on the ground.

☐ Enmity between the serpent (representing Satan) and the woman's seed (people and, ultimately, Christ) would exist. Constant warfare between people and the evil one would only be overcome through Christ (Romans 16:20; Hebrews 2:14). Genesis 3:15 is the first hint of the need for a Messiah. (Satan is told, "he will crush your head.")

☐ Pain in childbirth for the woman would be a constant reminder of the sin and fall of the human race.

☐ Marital and relational struggle was another consequence. Woman would desire man (perhaps in a manipulative way; see Genesis 4:7 where *desire* means, "to prompt evil"). So it might be read: "your desire will be to grab hold of him or control him, but he will rule over you." This destroyed the unity of Genesis 1:28, where together they would rule as partners, side by side, as equals over creation. Now the man would seek to rule over her, and she would seek to control him, something we have seen played out throughout history.

☐ The ground would be cursed, making humanity's work toilsome and difficult. The man and woman both worked before there was sin, so work is not the curse. Rather, the nature of work would change. It would now include great struggle.

☐ Physical death would now occur (Genesis 3:19: "to the dust you will return").

☐ Banishment from the Garden of Eden removed people from the perfection of creation that God had made. Verse 22: "He must not be allowed to reach out his hand and take also from the tree of life and eat, and live forever," may confuse readers. If someone raises the question, refer to a commentary or other resource for a detailed answer. Basically, God did not want humans to live forever in the painful condition of sin. Though he banished them (judgment) he had already begun to provide for their redemption (grace).

Note that the serpent, the woman and the man were all judged. But only the ground and the serpent were *cursed.* People often think that the pain woman would experience in childbirth was a curse—but it was not. The curse here was a strong pronouncement of judgment that had long-term implications and a sense of finality to it. In this case, the only way the curse will be overcome is when the entire world is redeemed and made whole again at the coming of Christ (Romans 8:19-20).

3. Flood. Most people are familiar with the flood story. Focus on the question listed. How long after the creation of the world did the flood happen? We are not sure. It was not the purpose of the writer to give those details.

4. Abraham's migration from Ur to Canaan. Briefly discuss how we are blessed through Abraham's seed, Christ. Review the map as listed.

5. Joseph and the slavery in Egypt. Joseph's story again reminds us that God will accomplish his redemptive purposes. Humanity cannot overcome the will of God, who will use even the most adverse circumstances to his advantage.

6. Moses and the exodus. Israel's slavery to Egypt and redemption by God are pictures of our sin and redemption through Christ. As the blood on the doorposts protected the Jews from the angel of death, the blood of Christ cleanses us from sin and keeps us from eternal death.

Trailmarkers (10 min.) These verses are here to show us how God uses normal people to carry out his plan. We are like the "famous" people of the Old Testament, who were very human and very ordinary. We too can be used of God in powerful ways.

Teamwork (15 min.) You can learn from what people draw. Watch for details. Ask each person to explain one of his or her drawings. You will gain insight to what they learned and why it was important to them. This exercise is designed to bring some creativity and fun to the study of history. The word for each event provides an overall theme; there are really no wrong answers. It is simply a way to associate a word with a picture and help people remember the event and its significance.

Reaching the Summit (5 min.) Help the group see that an understanding of biblical history and God's work through it shapes the way we see the world. These early themes remind us that God is the sovereign Creator who, despite our rebellion, has been gracious to provide a Redeemer. God is "for us" even when we have turned from him. The amazing history of the Bible is a constant reminder of God's grace revealed to a sinful people.

Next Session (3 min.) The nation of Israel enters the Promised Land with hope and some fear, but under God's rule. Give the group an exciting insight into next session, a kind of "wait until you see what is next!" What lies ahead are some of the greatest demonstrations of God's power and the unfolding plan for the coming of Christ.

Close in Prayer (10 min.) There is a great deal for which we can give thanks. Like Adam, Eve, Abraham, Sarah, Joseph and Moses, we are fallen creatures who doubt and rebel. Recognize God's forgiveness and grace and ask for wisdom to avoid mistakes that others have made. Ask that God will help you realize your brokenness, but that he will also remind you that you are filled with possibilities for great love and impact if you will follow him.

Session 3. Conquest, Kingdom, Captivity & Preparation.
Introduce the Session (1 min.) Go over the purpose and goal.

Purpose: To grasp the range of biblical events that surround the rise and fall of Israel's kingdom in the Old Testament world, a period that lasted nearly one thousand years.

Goal: To learn to identify major events and key figures in the history of Israel leading to the close of the Old Testament era and preparation for coming of Jesus.

Establishing Base Camp (10 min.) There may be some sensitive stories here. For example, some of the biggest events that impacted both sides of my family are immigration to the United States in the nineteenth century from Europe. Between my wife and me, my father is the only one of our four parents who finished college. Two did not even start college. My exposure to educational opportunities as a baby boomer has greatly enhanced the development of my family compared to just a few generations before.

Mapping the Trail (10 min.) Take a moment to tell that group that we will cover a lot of history in this one short session. Knowing key dates is helpful, but make it clear to the group that memorizing dates is not what is most important. The main thrust should be on the rise and fall of the nation based on the devotion of the leaders as well as the people. The question here is designed to help people anticipate the events by looking at the expectations they have. Will Israel survive? Will God be with us? Will I prosper? These questions were probably in the mind of every Jew when crossing the Jordan.

Beginning the Ascent (30 min.) The history of the ancient world contains records of many "people movements" or migrations. Israel's journey from Egypt to Canaan and their occupation is just one of them. Israel's experience is however different. At some point in the study you might want to read Deuteronomy 4:32-40 to the group and show them how unique and powerful God is, and how great a love he has for Israel.

Following this momentous occasion, their history can be divided into four eras:

1. Conquest and occupation—350 years. God's command to enter the Promised Land and kill the inhabitants has always raised questions for people. Some may see this as genocide or "ethnic cleansing." How do Christians respond to that charge? Is this the same God who appears in the New Testament in the person of Jesus? Don't forget that God is a God of justice. It is his nature to love but also to execute justice and divine wrath because of sin (the same wrath Christ took upon himself at the cross). He is patient to a point at which his just and holy character must be satisfied. (Remember the account of Sodom and Gomorrah, and the flood. In each case God was patient and allowed people many opportunities to repent.) People who had deliberately and repeatedly turned from God to practice wickedness inhabited the land of Canaan. Israel became the instrument of his judgment.

During the period of the Judges, a cycle repeats itself throughout the book. The people sin, an oppressor (another nation) is used by God to humble Israel, then they repent, and finally God raises up a deliverer (a judge) to lead his people out of bondage or destruction. Sin, oppression, repentance, deliverance: this is the book of Judges.

Note: Judges were not what we call "judges" today. They were military or political leaders, not interpreters of the law.

2. Development of the monarchy (kingdom)—120 years. While having a king might seem "natural," it was clearly not God's intention. Deuteronomy 17:14-20 prophesies that they will want a king. 1 Samuel 8:7 indicates that such a desire is a rejection of God's reign. Saul was the perfect example of what not to have in a king. Outwardly he looked like a leader, but his heart was not pure. Other kings, like Solomon, were the kind that Moses warned against in Deuteronomy 17:16-17: "he must not acquire a great number of horses . . . he must not take many wives." David also violated this guideline.

3. Division and exile/captivity—350 years. Just before the division, a prophet tells Jeroboam that God is going to give him leadership over ten tribes. God knew that Rehoboam would oppress the people and give them a reason to rebel. Over the following centuries there were many bad kings and many good ones. It is important to recognize that even the best kings (fathers) often had sons who rebelled against them and God.

First and Second Chronicles places emphasis on the history of the southern two tribes, Judah and Benjamin. First and Second Kings includes a wider selection of kings from the northern ten tribes, often called Israel. (The southern kingdom is called Judah).

4. Restoration and preparation—150 years. God gave Israel and Judah every opportunity to return to him. The conclusion of 2 Chronicles (36:14-23) explains the sad reasons for the captivity and the prospect of the return from exile. Reasons for the captivity include

- a persistent worship of idols and refusal to turn to the true God
- a repeated rejection of God's messengers, the prophets
- a refusal to give the land its sabbath rest

The applications here are straightforward. Any system that does not have God at the core produces idolatry. Men and women cannot continue to reject the message of God's Word and expect to avoid judgment, and God will see that the principles of his Word are practiced even if he must use extreme means to accomplish his will.

Leaders have a tremendous impact—both for good and bad. If you were to review the kings of Israel, the ten northern tribes, you would find very little good to say about any of them. The sad chorus repeated over and over is "he did evil in the eyes of the LORD."

The Bible is not a text book on world history, but it does faithfully record interaction between Israel and its neighbors, much of which is military campaigns. These are listed for your reference and background as a leader but are not necessarily for group discussion.

Empire	Duration	Interaction with Israel
Egypt	2000-760	Genesis/Exodus/Kings/Chronicles repeated attacks during kingdom era
Assyria	760-612	Kings/Chronicles; northern tribes taken into captivity in 722 B.C.
Babylon	612-539	Chronicles/Daniel Jerusalem plundered (606, 597 B.C.), then burned at captivity in 586
Persia	539-331	Chronicles/Daniel/Ezra/Nehemiah
Greece	331-146	Not recorded in the Bible
Rome	146 B.C.—A.D. 430	The entire New Testament era

Read the quote by Leon Wood under "Gaining a Foothold." Allow the group to reflect again on the purpose of knowing God's historical record in the Bible and how we benefit from reading it.

Trailmarkers (10 min.) The amount of material included in the Old Testament is enormous. Encourage group members to use the listed passages for extra reading and future study. It is not necessary to read every passage during the lesson; use your time wisely to cover the broad range of material without getting bogged down.

We highlighted the two passages as possible memory verses because of their great impact. Take a few minutes to ponder these key verses, and if time allows, start memorizing one of them in teams or pairs.

Teamwork (15 min.) The bookmark idea in option one provides a chance to be creative. If someone turns up something especially great, you might want to photocopy it for the group.

The second option is an interactive way to get some facts in people's heads without burdening them with details or expecting them to memorize dates and names. It is a fun review and should be treated that way. Make sure that each question has a personal application portion or follow-up question. We don't want to simply have a trivia contest. This brief exercise is designed to cover *major* events, dates and people so that everyone gets a better handle on the flow of Old Testament history. Remember that knowledge for knowledge's sake makes people proud and arrogant (see Proverbs 16:18).

Reaching the Summit (5 min.) Make sure you review the repeated expressions of God's grace to the Israelites. In spite of how evil kings and common men may have been, God repeatedly orchestrated great spiritual recoveries for Israel. Help group members understand the concept of grace as an undeserved and often refused gift.

Next Session (3 min.) The life of Christ is the focus of the next session. These questions are aimed at showing the reader how important his life is. The amount of material covering the three-and-a-half years of Jesus' ministry is extensive compared to the amount of material for the two-thousand-plus years of Old Testament history. And the Passion Week, the last week of his earthly life, takes center stage. Ask members to reflect on the importance of his life by reading through one entire Gospel this week. Mark is the shortest and most succinct, Luke the longest but most descriptive, John the most theological and profound, and Matthew the most Jewish and prophetic.

Close in Prayer (10 min.) Learning "about" Old Testament history is different from learning "from it." Prayers for group needs should not be ignored, but some time can be spent on the need for all of us to learn and grow in character and in gratitude for God's great work of grace.

Session 4. The Life of Christ.
Introducing the Session (1 min.) Go over the purpose and goal.

Purpose: To better understand the Bible and apply it to our lives through gaining a picture of the basic flow of New Testament events.

Goal: To identify the three seasons of Jesus' public ministry and the three primary expeditions that carried the good news to cities throughout the Mediterranean world.

Establishing Base Camp (10 min.) Focus here on helping people see that God's purpose for them is personal and filled with potential for impacting other's lives. It is important to have a sense of accomplishment in life, in fulfilling the mission God has given to us. Paul felt this in 2 Timothy 4:7, where he says he has fought the good fight and finished the course.

What process or exercises could help group members discover a sense of passion for life and ministry? You might make comments such as, "Having a passion or sense of calling is certainly biblical." And, "Discovering our passion means we must look deep inside." Suggest that each member ask, "What clues do I see in my life that indicate what my passion might really be?" Passion is that which thrills and excites you and can be directed toward God's greater purpose and work in the world. An artist paints for the glory of God, a teacher tries to inform minds and change hearts, and a mechanic desires to build something with integrity and quality that will serve others.

Mapping the Trail (10 min.) Begin by helping the group focus on Jesus' last week and the defining moments of his life. What do they understand about his work and mission? If they get stuck, you might find it valuable to have selected a few events that demonstrate his redemptive mission rather than simply his miraculous power.

When considering significant events, responses might include Jesus' conversation with Nicodemus concerning new life (John 3), his offer of forgiveness to the woman at the well (John 4) or the radical act of service in washing the disciples' feet. Others may include the cross, Jesus' miracles or his teaching.

The focus of the Gospels on Jesus' last week indicate that they are not designed as traditional biographies—rather, they are written as redemptive biographies. The Gospels include those events and teachings that have the most bearing on God's work of reaching the lost and building the kingdom. Matters concerning Jesus' life as a child or a carpenter are omitted because of the focus on Jesus as the promised Messiah.

Beginning the Ascent (30 min.) Jesus' public ministry began with his baptism and the forty-day temptation in the wilderness. It ended with his final week of teaching and his death, burial and resurrection in Jerusalem.

Phase one. Immediately before Jesus "went public," John the Baptist spent six months preparing for Jesus. During these early months, Jesus performed his first public miracle, turning water into wine (John 2). He later drove the moneychangers out of the temple area. He then withdrew to Galilee, traveling through Samaria, where he spoke to the woman at the well (John 4)

Jesus was baptized by John in the Jordan River. They probably did not know each other well if at all, even though John was Jesus' relative (Elizabeth was Mary's cousin, aunt or other—we do not know). Their families did not live close together. Elizabeth lived in the Judean hill country while Mary was in Nazareth in Galilee (Luke 1:39), and John had spent much time in the wilderness while Jesus was a carpenter. If they had any contact as children, perhaps at one of the religious festivals, they had changed so much that John did not recognize him. Or perhaps this refers to John simply not knowing Jesus as Messiah (John 1:29-34). When you read the full account in Luke 4, you get the bigger picture.

Jesus' temptation served to give him spiritual strength even though it caused him physical weakness. Overcoming Satan in this deprived condition and remaining in close contact with his heavenly Father through prayer and solitude allowed the Holy Spirit to work powerfully through him. God often used the wilderness to teach those he had chosen (Moses, Elijah and John the Baptist are good examples). And he uses his Spirit to teach us there as well.

Phase two. As you read through this together, help the group see that Jesus had both a public ministry of preaching, teaching and miracles and a more focused ministry of development with the twelve as a group. Peter, James and John were his closest companions. They were present with him at the transfiguration (Mark 9:1) and in the Garden of Gethsemane (Mark 14:33), and they are mentioned as pillars of the early church (Galatians 2:9).

The Apostles

1. Peter	5. Philip	9. James, son of Alphaeus
2. Andrew	6. Bartholomew	10. Simon the Zealot
3. James	7. Matthew	11. Judas son of James
4. John	8. Thomas	12. Judas Iscariot

(Note: Judas Son of James is "Thaddeus" in Matthew 10 and Mark 3.)

Phase three. Note here that Jesus had to go to Jerusalem (Luke 9:51; 13:22) to fulfill his mission of teaching and ultimately his crucifixion. Jerusalem was the center of religious life for Jews and they traveled there at least once a year as part of the Jewish Passover celebration. People also came for other feasts and to bring sacrifices to the temple.

Phase four. This final week of ministry is the culmination of the mission. Help the group understand the significance of this week and how Jesus maintained a true focus on his ultimate mission despite many challenges, frustrations and threats. What does this say about the determination we should have about our own mission?

 Trailmarkers (10 min.) Help the group discuss this chart and ask for any observations they have. If you can, form partners and do some memory work.

Teamwork (15 min.) The purpose in option one is to provide a concise but meaningful overview of Jesus' life. Encourage creativity in a "reporter's" style, but make sure the facts are maintained. For option two remember the emphasis is not on artistic ability. Enjoy interacting with each other's creations. Even those who are reluctant at first will find an interest in adding their picture to the discussion once they have seen a few others. Encourage the group to create mental pictures, and thank them for their courage in sharing their artwork with the group.

Reaching the Summit (5 min.) Encourage the group to see past the dates and times to the significance of the events. Congratulate them and remind them of the freedom this information will give them as they read the Bible for themselves. Reflect on the impact that the life of Christ has on us today and why it is important to see the facts concerning his life and ministry. The eyewitness accounts of the Gospels lend great credibility to the New Testament history.

Next Session (5 min.) Acts 1:8 shows Jesus' charge to the church. Much like Matthew 28:18-20, this passage describes Jesus' desire to expand the mission long after he is gone.

Close in Prayer (10 min.) Ask God to guide you in your effort to use your time wisely. The life of faith requires us to face many challenges. What tools and resources will be equip us to successfully follow Christ?

Session 5. The Church.
Introducing the Session (1 min.) Go over the purpose and goal.

Purpose: To understand the events that laid the ground for the expansion of the church and the spreading of the gospel, as Christ commanded. Like the other lessons in this study guide, our understanding of the Bible and application of its principles to our lives will be enhanced through understanding the basic flow of New Testament events.

Goal: When the lesson is finished, we will be able to identify the three primary expeditions that carried the good news to cities throughout the Mediterranean world.

Establishing Base Camp (10 min.) This discussion is designed to focus people not simply on the facts about the church but on the life of the church. Emphasize to people that this is who we are. Of all the sections in this study, this one should arouse some passion. A look at the early church should give us an appreciation for what it took to build and protect it.

As you answer the questions, make sure this is not a gripe session about how bad the church is at times. If people are strongly negative here, that's okay because it is their opinion. But don't dwell there. You might ask, "So how has this affected your ministry today? Do you see yourself working to bring life to the church so it will not repeat the same mistakes?"

For those with no church background, listen carefully to how they viewed (or still view) the church.

Mapping the Trail (10 min.) Guide the group through Acts 2:42-47 and help them identify the life-giving aspects of the early church. As you do this, you might ask or challenge, "So what keeps us from becoming this kind of church today? Why do we think this was only a historical phenomenon?" The early enthusiasm and heart of the church was contagious and explosive, contributing to high growth (three thousand added on one day, growing to five thousand men plus families by Acts 4:4). We can recapture some of that enthusiasm. This is about heart and focus. The early church had lots of problems (sin began early, as we see in Acts 5). But its leaders continued to teach and model Jesus' way of life, and the church continued to have impact.

Beginning the Ascent (30 min.) Read this section to the group and let them feel a flow for the expansion of the church. Remind them that this took only about thirty years. Paul's ministry lasted about twenty years; Peter's lasted about thirty.

Allow one or two members to share their testimony. If you have time, everyone can briefly (in two or three minutes) give an overview of how they came to faith. You could also do this in pairs if you want people to tell a longer story to each other. Watch your time here. Ask what role key people played in their lives to bring them to faith. The exciting thing about the church is that we can have a team effort in evangelism and discipleship. Paul is a prominent figure, but he had lots of help and encouragement from Barnabas and later Luke, Timothy, Priscilla and Aquila, Lydia, and a host of others.

Paul's three journeys set the stage for most of the early church expansion. He was a high-energy man with a unique conversion and training experience that gave him a sense of urgency and confidence to boldly and repeatedly preach the gospel. But he was more than an evangelist; he established churches and helped them grow. His letters are not simply doctrinal lectures but are filled with comfort and prayers for new believers facing persecution, sin and fear. His basic pattern was to preach, organize new converts, move on to another city, and then, in most cases, return later to encourage believers and handle disputes or misunderstandings. Once a church was established, he wrote letters to minister to and guide them.

The question about starting a church is designed to help us feel some of what Peter, Paul, Priscilla and Aquila, and others felt when they started new churches. Here we want to focus the discussion on expectations, resources, the work of the Holy Spirit, obstacles, leadership, evangelism and discipleship.

Finally, the discussion about our own call and commitment is designed to help us all be grateful for the price paid by early Christians to establish the church Christ died for. We should each have a commitment to the local church and its mission. Are we as dedicated to our church as these leaders were to theirs? Are we willing to forgo some of life's comforts or activities to spend more time building the church? Do we really see ourselves as ministers of the gospel?

Trailmarkers (10 min.) Read through the verses and briefly discuss them. Encourage to group to memorize a verse about the church. Give them a few minutes to begin this process either alone or in pairs.

Teamwork (15 min.) Key themes and characteristics of the church are found in this passage. Paul challenges them here to live out their calling in Christ. You can divide into smaller groups or teams as suggested in the study, or do this as a large group. It depends on the time you have. Here are some characteristics to look for in your discussion.

Topic	Verses
How to Treat One Another	1-2
Unity of the Church	3-6
Diversity of Spiritual Gifts	7-8
Purpose of Spiritual Gifts	11-13
Maturity of the Church	14-16

These are categories. Members will probably be much more specific. For example someone might say, "The church is supposed to teach people."

A follow-up question might address how your group can reflect some of these principles. That will help them to see that they are "a church" in some form because they are the body of Christ gathered together. It will also keep them from looking to the leaders of your church to do it for them. It is easy to talk about "them" and how "they" can change the church. But we are the people of God, and must take some responsibility in the body.

Reaching the Summit (5 min.) The story of Christianity's spread is exciting. People everywhere "hear" God's message in the universe (Psalm 8; Romans 1:18-20), but they cannot believe in Jesus until they learn about him (Romans 10:14-18). There is a part we can play in the drama of redemption as God seeks the lost.

Next Session (3 min.) We will bring together all that we have learned about the geography and chronology in the next session. Here you will see how it all works together to provide a rich, full description of God's unfolding plan in the world!

Close in Prayer (10 min.) Thank God for the church, the early apostles and leaders who sacrificed so much for her, and ask God to bless your church. Seek to become an active participant in the redemptive drama.

Session 6. Putting It All Together.

Introduce the Session. This meeting has a different format from the others. It is primarily a team project, followed by prayer and celebration. Enjoy it and have some fun as you bring your learning into focus.

There are a few different options described in the session for "putting it all together" in a creative or interactive way. History, especially biblical history, is not boring when linked to life and explained with passion.

Go over the purpose and goal.

Purpose: To give group members the opportunity to create a big picture and use it to enrich their spiritual life through applying Bible lessons to life.

Goal: To give group members a renewed feel for the scope of biblical history and its environment. Group members will be able to identify major events, people and the places in the Old and New Testaments.

Establishing Base Camp (10 min.) Help the group see that events have a defining characteristic in our lives. And also help them see that the same event that inspired people thousands of years ago can still inspire us today. There is nothing more exciting than the story of a changed life and seeing the hand of God at work in profound ways.

Use this session to create a framework for your group that will spur them on to a lifetime of Bible reading and study as they follow Christ.

Mapping the Trail (10 min.) The point of this question is to challenge people to realize that our experience and setting can color what we see and how we interpret it. This is why the Bible is a unique book. The perspective of the many writers is consistent, even though they wrote from many places and were separated by hundreds of years. (See *Foundations* and *Interpretation* in the Bible 101 series for further study of the integrity of the history of the Word and to understand what it teaches.) It is because of the diversity of the biblical writings that we can trust the Scripture and have a broad, historical picture of the truth.

 Teamwork (60 min.) Option one is the "study and present" option. People will work for the period of time allowed and then present an overview to the group. This will help members focus on the significant people and events instead of trivia. And it will provide people with the experience of putting the story in their own words. You should probably allow them five to seven minutes to present their work. One person could be chosen from each team, or team members could each take part as they choose. Keep it fun, watch the time and emphasize the impact of events on the life of God's people. A few follow-up questions from you or others would be appropriate to each presentation.

If you choose option two, ask someone in the group who has some basic drawing ability to draw a map of the ancient Near East on a large piece of cardboard or paper. Ask that person to color sections, mark cities and places. You will need to make sure there are enough markers. (Ask several group members to bring some in case one forgets or can't make the meeting last minute.) If you have limited time, draw the map ahead of time and perhaps list the cities and regions on it. Then the group can more quickly get to the people and events, discussing the impact of these.

Also provide 3 × 5 cards, perhaps in at least two colors (or ask others to bring these). Use one color for Old Testament events and characters and a different color for New Testament events and characters. Use the cards as mentioned to mark places and events or stories on the map.

You could also try a third option that is not mentioned in the study session. Set up a quiz game. Create a series of cards (by cutting 3 x 5 cards in half) with names and places to use in quizzing each other. The goal is to reinforce the lessons from the study. Focus on major, meaningful events from the charts above. We don't want to learn trivia. We want to have an understanding of the framework in which the Scripture is set so that we can grasp the import of what we read.

Whatever option you choose, keep it festive and light. Encourage the group to realize how much they have learned and how it ties together. God has been at work, and is at work today, all around the world. His work is independent of culture, geography, money or the lack of it, even education and sophistication.

Encourage the creative members to go all out with their artwork. Engage the organizational and administrative folks to keep order and plot travel routes, and make sure the place names are accurate. Include modern geographic notations as well, such as Iran and Iraq. (Egypt is still the same!) You might want to have an atlas of today's world handy. Show people how today's Middle Eastern countries line up with biblical ones. Someone familiar with current events can add some commentary along the way. This will help people better understand why some of the tensions exist there and how various religious groups (Jew, Christian, Muslim) view the land and its history.

 Reaching the Summit (5 min.) Step back and take a look at your work.

Thank the group for the effort and persistence to tackle such a big task. Regardless of the option chosen, the ability to gain an overview of the Bible in this way is invaluable and will bear fruit in your study of the Word of God for years to come.

Next Session (3 min.) Choose another study from the Bible 101 series or elsewhere. Perhaps a break is needed for a celebration night or a dinner followed by a worship and prayer time. Use wisdom to discern what is the best next step for your group.

You might encourage group members to develop a Bible reading plan—not necessarily one book per week if they are not accustomed to doing so.

Close in Prayer (10 min.) Thank God for the marvel of all that you have studied about the Bible—the cultural world, the life stories therein and the power of the truth. Affirm and celebrate one another for the hard work, asking God to use it for spiritual growth.